What Scissors Taught Me

Denise Létienne

 FriesenPress

One Printers Way
Altona, MB R0G 0B0
Canada

www.friesenpress.com

Copyright © 2022 by Denise Létienne
First Edition — 2022

ISBN
978-1-03-915161-1 (Hardcover)
978-1-03-915160-4 (Paperback)
978-1-03-915162-8 (eBook)

1. BIOGRAPHY & AUTOBIOGRAPHY, PERSONAL MEMOIRS

Distributed to the trade by The Ingram Book Company

To every three-year-old that dreams of becoming a hairstylist,
dream big.
To my hairstyling peers who continue to dream,
take that needed vacation time,
get monthly massages,
buy great pairs of comfortable shoes,
practice yoga.
Seriously! It's saving me!

To my mom and dad residing in heaven,
I miss you.

scis·sors
/ˈsizərz/
noun
1. an instrument used for cutting cloth, paper, and other thin material, consisting of two blades laid one on top of the other and fastened in the middle so as to allow them to be opened and closed by a thumb and finger inserted through rings on the end of their handles.

Fun Fact
Leonardo da Vinci has often been credited with inventing scissors—he used the device for cutting canvas—but the household tool predates his lifetime by many centuries. Nowadays, it's hard to find a household that doesn't have at least one pair.

Folklore and Superstition
More than one expectant mother has placed a pair of scissors beneath her pillow at night somewhere toward the end of her ninth month of pregnancy. Superstition says that this will "cut the cord" with her baby and prompt labor.

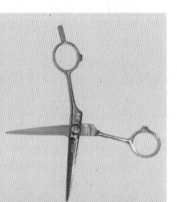

And here's another tall tale: Don't hand those scissors to your best friend. Place them on any available surface and let your friend pick them up. Otherwise, you risk severing your relationship. Some say that those scissors languishing in your catch-it-all drawer can help keep evil spirits out of your home. Hang them by one handle near your door so they form a version of a cross.

Ancient Scissors

The ancient Egyptians used a version of scissors as long ago as 1500 B.C. They were a single piece of metal, typically bronze, fashioned into two blades that were controlled by a metal strip. The strip kept the blades apart until they were squeezed. Each blade was a scissor. Collectively, the blades were scissors, or so rumour has it. Through trade and adventure, the device eventually spread beyond Egypt to other parts of the world.

The Romans adapted the Egyptian's design in 100 A.D., creating pivoted or cross-blade scissors that were more in line with what we have today. The Romans also used bronze, but they sometimes made their scissors from iron as well. Roman scissors had two blades that slid past each other. The pivot was situated between the tip and the handles to create a cutting effect between the two blades when they were applied to various properties. Both Egyptian and Roman versions of scissors had to be sharpened regularly.

Scissors Enter the 18th Century

Although the actual inventor of scissors is hard to identify, Robert Hinchliffe, of Sheffield, England, should be rightfully acknowledged as the father of modern scissors. He was the first to use steel to manufacture and mass-produce them in 1761—more than 200 years after da Vinci's death.

Pinking shears were invented and patented in 1893 by Louise Austin of Whatcom, Washington. As Austin noted in her patent application, which was granted on Jan. 1, 1893:

"With my improved pinking scissors or shears, the pinking or scalloping can always be made uniform and in line; and it is performed by cutting continuously through the fabric from end to end or edge to edge; thus, the work is very rapidly done, and, where the fabric is severed, two scalloped edges will be produced at the same operation."

Scissors in Print

Scissors have been mentioned in print over the years. In "Emar, Capital of Aštata in the Fourteenth Century BCE," a 1995 article published in the journal *The Biblical Archaeologist*, authors Jean-Claude Margueron and Veronica Boutte included this passage:

"Besides ceramics, occasionally collected in large quantities, the houses produced stone and metallic objects illustrating both day-to-day needs and the activities of city merchants: beer filters, containers, arrow and javelin heads, scales of armor, needles and scissors, long nails, bronze scrapers, millstones, mortars, many kinds of grindstones, pestles, various tools and stone rings."

And in an entire book describing the history of the cutting tool, called, appropriately, "A Story of Shears and Scissors: 1848–1948," author Don Wiss described the history of the implement:

"Egyptian bronze shears of the Third Century B.C., a unique object of art. Showing Greek influence although with decoration characteristic of Nile culture, the shears are illustrative of the high degree of craftsmanship which developed in the period following Alexander's conquest of Egypt. Decorative male and female figures, which complement each other on each blade, are formed by solid pieces of metal of a different color inlaid in the bronze shears."

"Sir Flinders Petrie ascribes the development of cross-bladed shears to the First Century. In the Fifth Century, the scribe Isidore of Seville describes cross-bladed shears or scissors with a center pivot as tools of the barber and tailor."

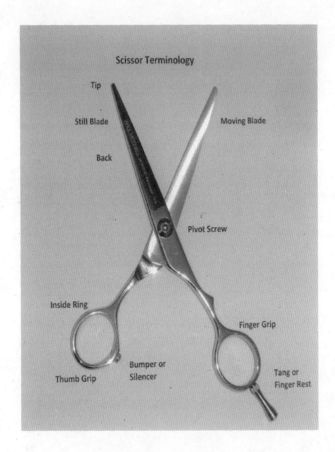

The above trivia and fun facts about scissors was taken from "Who Invented Scissors?", written by Mary Bellis, ThoughtCo, Jan. 24th, 2021, thoughtcompany.com/who-invented-scissors-4070946

"Are you giving the same advice over, and over, and over again to clients, patients, pupils, interns, or friends? If the answer is yes, you should probably write a book about whatever it is that you keep repeating." *Gudjon Bergmann - Quotestats.com*

And So It Begins

As far back as I can remember, I wanted to be a hairstylist. As a young child, I cut hair on every single doll and Barbie that was deemed mine in the house, and the occasional doll that didn't belong to me. Anything with hair, really. I received a toy monkey as a gift one year, and even that little guy couldn't escape my mom's scissors. Yes, in the 1960s, I was allowed to play with those. I also had a cute little ironing board, with an iron that plugged into a wall socket and heated up. My doll clothes were always extremely neat and tidy. At the age of three, and possibly younger, my mother would let me stand on the couch, lean into the back of it, and use one of her hairbrushes to brush her hair while she was knitting or did a household chore, like folding laundry while watching something on television. There wasn't much choice in those days. We had three English channels and one French channel available to us. We had a giant (to me) TV console; the screen might have been 28 inches tops! This large mahogany cabinet also had a turntable in it, and large speakers built in on either side. My dad stored a small collection of records in the designated slots provided, mostly French artists like Maurice Chevalier, Edith Piaf, Mireille Mathieu, or my mom's favourites - Dean Martin, Bing Crosby, and Andy Williams.

Mom sometimes allowed this game of brushing her hair to go on for what seemed like hours, while she watched one of her shows, or more often, let me watch one of mine... The Friendly Giant, Mr. Dress-Up, or Chez Hélène. I was her fifth daughter. Blessed was I to have an attentive mom, with my four older siblings all out of the house, at work or school. I had her all to myself! She was 42 when she gave birth to me and stayed home to raise all of us until I was seven years old. She told me often that I was her "jambe de bois"... her "wooden leg" that would keep her young and standing for a very long time. She also told me that her wish was that one of her daughters would become a nurse, one would become a hairstylist, and one a secretary. A sign of the times. The other request was for all of us to be happy and marry a nice man with a good job. Another sign of the times.

I have several hobbies. Cuddling up to read a good book is something I have done since I was a child. One of my recent reads was Michelle Obama's memoir, Becoming. Her words are eloquently written, and very quickly, she struck a chord with me with her valued opinions. On the very first page of the Preface, she says, "One of the most useless questions an adult can ask a child is, 'What do you want to be when you grow up?' As if growing up is finite. As if at some point you become something and that's the end." I agree! I used to be guilty of asking this question to my many nieces and nephews, or any other child that I shared time with for that matter. I, as a child, was also asked this question numerous times. The interesting thing about me, as it may very well be for others, is that I have turned two of my childhood dreams into my reality. I cannot remember a day in my life when I wasn't thinking about hairstyling and teaching as a career. I never attended kindergarten, so as a five-year-old, in the basement of our family home,

I would set myself up on a little handed-down table and chair set, with pencils and paper, maybe a few crayons, and some chalk. The chalk was so that I could write on our unfinished concrete walls mimicking a chalkboard while teaching my dolls everything that I knew about hair at that time in my life. Two loves in my life, hairstyling and teaching, became my adult reality.

As the end of my grade twelve high school year approached, several of my girlfriends had already registered for hairstyling school. As tempting as it was to join them, I decided to look for work instead, to save money for school by working for one year. I was living at home with my parents and was way too comfortable to move out on my own. My parents supported me in living at home while working to achieve my dream job, so their love solidified my plan. Those were the good ol' days, where you went door-to-door to establishments to drop off a paper resumé for a job that you saw posted in the weekend newspaper. Having graduated in June of that year and being quite comfortable with no responsibilities while working part-time in the kitchen of a hospital, my dad sat me down in the month of October to discuss the fact that it was time to either move out or get a job. It's funny how this weird threat worked. I got dressed the following Monday morning, dropped off three resumés at three of the largest insurance companies in the city and received phone calls from all three of them for interviews. Another sign of the times… entry jobs aplenty. I said yes to one, and that was that. That initial interview was followed up by a second interview, and there I was, all grown up with my first full-time job, living at home with a happy dad and a proud mom. This one-year plan turned into nine years of pay raises, promotions, moving up the ladder in different departments, marriage, buying a house, suddenly needing the paycheck to pay for groceries, and finally leaving the company at the age of twenty-seven to get myself into hairstyling, the career that I had been dreaming of since the age of three. I didn't miss one day of class, mostly because I loved everything that I was learning, and partially because one month into schooling, I became pregnant with my daughter. I needed to complete this education on time, and I did.

Several years into my hairstyling career, I was cutting a friend's hair in my newly built salon when we burst into laughter, causing all other stylists and clients to turn their heads and look at us. We were loud and out of control. My business partner at the time turned to us and asked, "What kind of party are you having over there?" My client and I continued to belly-laugh with tear-filled eyes. He and I happened to be talking about many things, including personal and professional funny stories. "You've got a book in you somewhere," he declared. We then had a serious conversation about a book coming to fruition. We decided at that moment that I would title the book "Behind the Chair," and the plan was to have a tabletop book of some sort, relaying short stories of many who sat in my chair. As luck would have it, a genius industry professional started a web-based business for the hairstyling community called… you guessed it "BehindtheChair.com." The site is brilliant, sharing all kinds of industry information. I was so depleted when I got wind of this "title steal" (even though I acknowledged it was indeed a fantastic resource) that I gave up on the idea of ever writing my book.

I have been told by many others over the years that I should write a book. My eighth-grade teacher saw a skill in me that I didn't understand at the time and encouraged me to continue with my writing. So, I did just that at various times in my life. I also took to writing a two-page monthly newsletter to update clients on what was going on in the salon. I did this for many years for two different salons. I loved the creativity this activity allowed me and was often complimented on my writing. Life progressed and the inclination to write a book passed. And in all honesty, who the heck has time to write a book?

Fast forward to 2020. Like so many others, I bought a new Kitchen-Aid, making bread and cookies, and also dove into self-help things during the COVID19 pandemic and our multiple regional lockdowns. So, here I am, living my "Best Decade Ever" thanks to Mel Robbins. Look her up! With this motivational speaker's encouragement, many people are diving into dreams that they never imagined they would accomplish, me included. There has been a book in this head of mine for a very long time.

The many lessons hairdressing has taught me are found within these pages. My dream career has included much joy, many struggles, challenges to spare, a need to listen, many opportunities for empathy, sometimes a need to dig deep and find a truckload of patience, a definite need for physical and mental strength, a strong sense of humour and most of all, a love for people.

I hope you can savour the pages of this book, whether it is on paper, e-reader or audible. They are my heart! It took me some time to finally realize that all I really needed was a new title.

"Don't you want to see what happens if
you don't give up?" *Nightbirde*

Let's Talk About Hair and a Few Other Things

B y and large, the thing I have always been passionate about when it comes to hairstyling is educating my clients, always making sure that they know as much about hair as I do. I sometimes feel that I share too much, so I speak and let people discard what they don't want to hang onto from their minds. I always ensure that they know and understand the products I use on their hair and why. This includes my reasons for mixing more than one colour to achieve their desired result, why I may be adding a few foils to their service, and the necessity of using styling agents at home. My goal is for each of my clients to have nice and easy hair days.

The structure of hair is an amazing thing to me. The first time I saw a microscopic picture of an individual strand of hair blew my mind. You could see the fibres of the cortex (inner layer of hair) and how the cuticle (outer layer of hair) has a slight resemblance to shingles on the roof of a house and protects everything that lives inside of that one strand of hair. The personal collection of slide photography was taken by one of my industry mentors, someone who held a BSc degree in Mathematics and Chemistry, and a Ph.D. in Physical Chemistry. His education gave him a phenomenal edge in this industry and the ability to participate in the development of stellar hair products for multiple manufacturers over the length of his career.

Hair is complex, composed mainly of fibrous keratin protein. Information on the structure of hair is a healthy-sized chapter in the textbooks. I don't want to bore you with all the details, but I do want to include a little bit about the hydrogen bonds that live in the cortex of your hair. These bonds are easily broken down by heat and water, therefore are affected when you wash your hair or use hot tools, such as curling irons, flat irons, hot rollers and other fun gadgets and waving tools. Hydrogen and salt bonds will be affected by the humidity in the air. Years ago, on a hot and humid summer day, a local weather reporter displayed a chart explaining the dew point of the frizz factor of hair. For me, it was the best forecast that I had ever seen. It was a great analogy and I completely related to it. The higher the dewpoint, the more moisture there is in the air. To the dewpoint of 10, hair was going to be sleek. To the dewpoint of 13, hair was going to be wavy, 16, curly, 18, frizzy and 21, well, a ponytail was recommended. This day was a curly-hair-kind-of-day.

Think of the bonds as a firm handshake. When water or heat hits your hair, the firm handshake loosens slightly. When your hair dries from washing or cools down from the use of a hot tool, the handshake becomes firm again, solidifying your new style. Hopefully, knowing this will, if anything, help explain why your hair looks the way it does while taking a stroll on a hot and humid day.

Hairstylists are often told, "I can't do my hair like this at home" or, "I wish that you could come to my house every day to do my hair for me." In the early stages of my career, I let those comments sink in and thought, "Yes! I am a hair magician!" The reality is that I want my clients to look great every single day of their lives, even if it is a sit-on-the-couch-and-do-nothing or a messy-bun kind of day. Back when French braids were worn by many, including myself, I used to kneel on the floor in front of my clients to give them a hands-on demonstration on how to manoeuvre their tresses to successfully make the braids. Alternately, I'd demonstrate on mannequin heads so that they could see the technique firsthand. The goal of a hairstylist is for the client to look their best every single day, especially when away from the salon. One of the best compliments I ever received was from a new client letting me know that she found me by stopping a stranger in a shopping mall to ask her who did her hair. She loved her colour and style so much that she followed her for a while and stopped her to get my information. Wow! My client was doing a fabulous job looking great that day! This was early in my career, when I wasn't really putting in the effort of educating my clients, so witnessing the result of a walking advertisement made me step up my game in this regard a lot more.

I can't remember there being a blow dryer in the house when I was younger. My mother had weekly appointments with her long-time hairdresser Leonie and my sisters all owned hood dryers from K-Mart for home use. Incidentally, some hairstylists don't like the word hairdresser, but the fact remains that we do dress the hair. It's an old-school term, and I still like it. I feel that some hairstylists believe that the word hairstylist is fancier or more important. I've been called worse things in my lifetime and am not offended by the term.

If I remember correctly, I just went to bed with wet hair when I was younger, and let my pillow soak up all the moisture. Today, there seems to be a tremendous overuse of flat irons, curling irons and various types of hot tools for styling purposes, and people are starting to use them at a younger age. When using a hot tool, it is recommended to use a thermal active spray, which is activated by the heat of the tool to protect the hair from the extreme heat of the tool and solidify the style that you want the tool to accomplish. When using a flat iron to straighten hair, place a small section of hair between the plates and glide the iron down from your scalp to the ends of your hair. If you are curling your hair with a flat iron by giving the plates of the iron a half-turn or more depending on the curl you want to achieve, you may want to begin midway down the shaft for a beachy wave look. Once the iron is out of your hair, give your hair a moment to cool down. No need to death-grip the iron or press the hair repeatedly. Repetition slightly confuses your hair. The hair bonds get hot, weaken, start to cool, and if you repeat the process, they get hit with more heat and don't know if they are supposed to be heating or cooling to take on another shape. This is the one reason that people think that their hair "never curls" or they need more heat. One slow pass is sufficient. Be methodical. A word of caution though: slow and steady is a great method. Too slow can absolutely melt your hair. There are many excellent professional hot tools for hairstyling, with some temperatures reaching up to 450°F. I cook chicken in my oven at 350°F! Imagine hitting your hair with an iron at 450°F! It's almost ridiculous unless you were blessed with extremely thick and coarse hair that requires a little bit more heat to control the waves and curls. The optimum temperature for hair, I find, is between 300 and 380°F, all dependent on hair texture and porosity. When using a hot tool on my own, very fine and colour-treated hair, my pre-set on the iron is 360°F and I don't sway from that. I have no need. Remember the chicken! And if you don't believe that hair can melt, I urge you to find a few videos on YouTube. Apparently, people like to show their horror on this media outlet, and one that I know of even made it as a guest on The Ellen Show.

Bobby pins are a staple in hair salons. They are the go-to for creating beautiful updos for all occasions. It is a small piece of metal with a flat side and a bumpy side. One of my all-time favourite updo hair gurus taught me that bobby pins should be put in the hair pointing upwards to support the "up" styles. He also taught that the "bumpy side grips and the flat side slips." This phrase has been ingrained in my mind for years and has helped me to achieve many successful updos, including on my head. Use as many pins as you need to support your style. If done right, it shouldn't require too many unless you have copious amounts of hair. Criss-crossing bobby pins to form an "X" is a good way to lock them into place and give your style stability. Finally, for the love of hairstyling, please don't use your two front teeth to separate and open the pin! Bobby pins are designed to hold whatever amount of hair that they can when being slid into the hair, as is. By prying it open, you are asking the pin to hold more hair than it can, and it will soon slide out of the hair and cause a collapsed hairstyle. Besides, opening the pin with your mouth is gross, and in my eyes, equal to licking the hair. Ewww!

I live where it can sometimes get down to -40° C in the winter. That's the same temperature in Fahrenheit. It's cold. And we adapt. It's the season when everyone comes in to declare that they have dandruff. For the most part, it is a dry scalp. A severe case of dandruff is referred to as seborrheic dermatitis, which I compare to cradle cap on babies' heads. Dandruff is a common skin disease that is comprised of itchy and patchy scales, redness on light skin and a lot of flakiness. If you suffer from a dry scalp, start by investing in a good shampoo and conditioning system. All shampoos and conditioning systems will clean your hair of product and debris. You will get what you pay for, however, so know what you are using on your head and why. I love this analogy used by another one of my mentors: if you bought a cashmere sweater or an expensive piece of clothing that required dry-cleaning only, you would not throw it in the washing machine with laundry soap. Similarly, your hair is a fabric, and you need to be using products that are conducive to the fabric on your head and the needs of your scalp. If your hair and scalp require specific products to soothe your ailments, be it curls, frizzy, fine hair, or dry scalp, invest in what is appropriate for your hair type. Note that shampooing your hair is not required daily. In my opinion, however, conditioners should be used every time you are wetting your hair. If you are jumping in the shower and skipping the shampoo, add a dab of conditioner to help smooth and protect your hair and scalp. Many stylists recommend applying conditioner to the ends of the hair only. To this point, if you are using a cleansing system particular to fine and/or thinning hair, or something to rectify dry scalp, the system likely has medicinal properties that would be effective if massaged directly into the scalp. Your professional hairstylist will be able to guide you to the products necessary for maintaining healthy hair and scalp, or direct you to a doctor if they feel that you require different attention or prescription medication.

Hair grows a quarter of an inch to a half-inch a month, and in some cases, hair can grow as fast as one inch a month. Going with a half-inch measure, hair, on average, grows approximately six inches in one year. Someone wearing their hair down to their waistline in length has hair that is potentially five to six, or maybe even seven years old. It has likely seen many colour processes, and a variety of hair products and has lived through much daily friction. The simple act of putting on and taking off clothing causes friction as the hair rubs up against the clothing. It's hard to get away from it. Laying your head down on a pillow and rolling around during the night causes friction. Why am I putting so much emphasis on friction? The reality is that rubbing the cuticle repetitively contributes to breaking down the ends of your hair. This causes split ends, technically known as trichoptilosis. Here is how you can help: after washing your hair, one's instinct may be to grab a towel and rub the hair vigorously. Please don't do this. Grab a towel and scrunch longer hair with the fingers and palms of your hands, squishing the hair gently. The towel will absorb the water. This method is especially beneficial to those with curly hair to enhance the curls. If you have straight and fine hair like mine, applying styling products and wrapping the wet hair back up in a towel, or a t-shirt for that matter, gives the option for something a little different, ending with unruly curls and messiness for a day or two.

Here's a word about dry shampoo: it's not really a shampoo. It's a product, typically a spray-in, designed to add texture to the hair on a day that it is not being washed. This product does have a slight ability to absorb oil on the scalp. It can also be used to add volume to the base of an updo. I'm not confident, however, that people who purchase dry shampoo read the instructions on how to use it. It's hard to shut off the hairstyling eye when out and about, and often, I have noticed dry shampoo residue in the hair of people walking by. Once you've sprayed your scalp with short bursts of dry shampoo, it is recommended to brush the product through your hair to ensure proper distribution. I will sometimes go as far as giving it a slight wipe with the corner of a towel. Most of these products have some form of talc in them, or a "sawdust" type of ingredient to enhance its benefits. Brush that stuff through your hair so that it isn't visible to the naked eye when out and about. It will work better for you if properly distributed in your hair.

Styling agents such as mousse, gel, pastes, oils, styling creams and hair sprays were all developed to help you in styling your hair and facilitating lasting hairstyles. Don't be afraid of them. Know what you are using and why. Let your stylist suggest what is right for you and let them guide you toward many great hair days.

It is very common as we age to lose hair. Don't panic. Our hair follicles begin to collect dihydrotestosterone (DHT). DHT builds up in the hair follicles and chokes out the hair bulb, which will no longer produce hair in that follicle, leading your head to a thinning scalp. Aside from natural aging, there are a few other reasons that may result in thinning locks. Using harsh shampoos with strong surfactants (surface active agent, also a fancy word for soap) may cause hair to dry and become brittle, causing breakage. At-home colour treatments, straightening systems, perming, or relaxing treatments can cause damage and breakage by not following instructions properly. Loosening the constant style of your ponytail to give your scalp a break and giving your head a rest from clip-in extensions are all helpful. Here is food for thought: if you are always pulling your hair off your face, maybe it's time for a shorter style. Other causes of thinning or hair loss are hereditary-pattern baldness, severe illness, or major surgery. Unhealthy eating habits, hormonal changes, various medical conditions, chemotherapy, and radiation treatments may also contribute to hair loss. There is unfortunately the "six of one and half a dozen of the other" situation, where sometimes, your body requires medication to fix one thing but then causes your hair to fall out. Arthritis, gout, some medications for depression and high blood pressure all have the potential for ill effects on hair. It's a vicious circle. Don't ever stop taking your medication. Do talk to your stylist about your hair fixes. Your stylist is your hair doctor and will advise you on what can be done, referring you to your medical professional for further help if required.

Here are a few bits of advice if you use a blow dryer. Blow dryers typically come with a nozzle attachment, which is designed to help concentrate the air in one location. This works great when using a brush while drying, as you can focus the air onto the brush to help style your hair. Remember that you can manipulate dry hair into a different shape, so if you are using a brush to style while drying, get most of the moisture out of the hair before using your brush. That nozzle is also movable. Instead of becoming a contortionist to manage your blow-dryer while drying your hair, you may just need to change the direction of the nozzle, say horizontally versus vertically. As a hairstylist, I am working directly above your head, which is a different perspective when using my tools on your head from when I use them on myself.

Let's get away from hair and talk about a few salon funnies... for those who have children: when it's time for your child's first haircut or any haircut for that matter, please don't speak the word, "cut" repetitively to them. Cutting at a young age is typically accompanied by hurt and blood, possibly a Band-Aid or two, and most likely a kiss on the booboo to make it feel better. When a child hears that they are scheduled for a hair "cut" their young minds sometimes associate it with pain and potential blood. They may also have had a few incidences at home where their hair was combed or brushed with some minor pain attached to the ordeal, which instinctively makes hairstylists "the bad person." Of course, this fear dissipates with time as children get to know the environment of the hair salon and the stylist. It may be a good idea to familiarize them with the process, possibly massaging their head to desensitize the feeling of combs and brushes running through their hair. Often with little "movers," no matter how well we wrap them in a towel and cape, they may get some hair clippings down their shirt, causing itching in the neck and back. Some kids won't allow us to place a cape or towel around their necks at all, resulting in a messy shirt at the end of their session. Bringing a spare shirt to change your child afterwards is never a bad idea. Bringing your own distractions in a favourite toy is always appreciated. And in case your hairstylist doesn't give out suckers or stickers, it's never a bad idea to reward your little tykes with a treat if you so choose. This is no different than when I take my grand pups for their nails, and they receive a cookie for good behaviour at the end of their appointment.

It's always great for you to bring along a photo of what you like in a hairstyle. However, I always explain to my clients that unless it's a picture of your friend, an aunt, or a sibling, the photos of the model in a magazine, on Pinterest or on Instagram are usually enhanced. Each model likely had special lighting effects to intensify the colour, and quite possibly a set of hands underneath her hair supporting it to make it look fuller. Most models in pictures don't wake up looking like their picture. I also examine both the model and the client's hair to compare textures. Admiring a super straight cut when your hair is naturally coarse and curly will require work to maintain the look. Bring photos if you wish and use them as a guide. Being flexible with the result is key. Sidenote here: taking a very dark brown or black head of hair to a light blonde is possible, but it likely won't happen overnight. Talk to your stylist about the possibility and process, or the reality.

Another side note: a stylist relies on their clients to make a living and believe me when I say that we all appreciate you! A stylist also books their day accordingly to the task at hand. Colour or balayage, which is a fabulous and artistic way of adding dimension to hair colour, will take two, three, and sometimes four hours or more to complete, and when we book your appointment, we allow for that time. On occasion, I have had people let me know that they need to be "done in an hour" as soon as they walk in the door. There are no shortcuts in hairstyling, no pun intended. Timing for service is what it is. We hope that you can relax once you've arrived and stay a while! Enjoy your YOU time and let us pamper you.

Hairstylists are a wonderful breed, and most are very caring and kind people. Nine out of ten stylists will likely say "it's ok", or "no problem" should you arrive a little late for your appointment. The challenge with that is that tardiness has the potential to delay their entire day. In the same way that doctors, dentists, lawyers, accountants, bankers, and other professionals rely on you to show up for your appointment on time, we appreciate the same. Of course, there is always the "sh*t happens" pile, but if clients are on the constant 20-to-30-minute-late-train, they stand a good chance of being de-hired from a salon. I am so thankful that I have "on-time" guests. As the last piece of advice on this topic, talk to your stylist about their no-show and cancellation policies.

It seems to be a human instinct that, while at the sink, you want to lift your head out of the neck rest to help us in the rinsing process. This is funny, and not funny. We know how to properly lift your head when it is in the sink and have been taught to support your neck to effectively give you a relaxing shampoo and conditioning service. When you lift your head, you risk water or chemical residue draining down the back of your body, resulting in wetting your entire backside. I would love for you to relax and let me guide your head up ever so slightly when it's time to rinse your nape. Closing your eyes while at the sink is also suggested. The main purpose of this is in the rare occasion that I let go of the sink hose while rinsing your hair, your eyes would be protected from water landing on them. The more serious scenario would be if particles of colour or other chemical service products entered your eyes, which could be harmful. I also feel that closed eyes are much more relaxing than looking up toward my nostrils while I'm working.

Years ago, I had the honour of experiencing a talk by Grace Ciracco, a bestselling author, and a gifted coach. During her presentation, she wrote the word passion on a board and then broke it down into three words: P-A-S-S, I, and O-N. She then created a heart shape around the word "I". I loved the symbolism. Your passion is something you love. Sharing your passion is passing on a piece of yourself and your knowledge to others. It was the best description of the word passion that I had ever witnessed, and it still holds profound meaning for me today. Teaching has always been about sharing knowledge, be it with my hairstyling peers, students, or salon guests. I now also hope that my shared knowledge may help someone who decided to pick up my book for something to read.

"Little things don't mean a lot. They mean absolutely everything." *Wayne Grund*

Little People

Some people become hairstylists and sign up to work in places that just service children. Without knowing any of these colleagues, I am going to go out on a limb and say that these are charming and brave souls with a whole lot of patience! Other people become hairstylists and for various reasons, don't even want to consider cutting children's hair. Some of the rationale may be that children's services don't bring in as much money in one sitting as an adult service would, or that children are sometimes difficult to deal with because, most of the time, they are a moving target. For sure, these little humans are a far cry from our non-communicative mannequin heads that, incidentally, I still practice on today. Mannequins are always cooperative. Children of all ages are sometimes afraid of going to a hairstylist, sitting in a big, weird chair with a stranger standing behind them, getting a haircut that they likely didn't ask for, or wanted for that matter, but mom and/ or dad insisted on it. There are many great reasons to freshen the look of your child... the first day of school, picture day, going to a birthday party, a special holiday, can't see your face anymore, no longer identifiable to your parent, or no longer distinct from your siblings to your grandparents, aunts, uncles, and neighbours. I love the story of one of my sisters, taking her son for a haircut when he was young. He had a full head of ravishing, thick, blonde curls. The hairstylist asked my sister, "Why are you cutting HER hair?" My sister replied, "That's why."

My favourite reason to cut and style a child's hair is when they have found well-hidden scissors at home, or scissors that were left in plain view for that matter, or sometimes their own kid scissors entice them, and rather than cutting paper, they took it upon themselves to take a chunk out of their hair. Typically, this occurs smack in the front of their head, inevitably, where everyone can see it. There is also the odd occasion where children get hold of a hair trimmer left sitting on a bathroom counter and shave a spot on top of their head, or somewhere else not so conspicuous. It is wherever their little arms and hands can reach. Over the course of my career, I've witnessed more than a few of these incidences. These mishaps just make me smile, and sometimes, laugh out loud. Until, one day, I came home from a Saturday workday, where I made my way to the bedroom to change out of my work clothes. On the way out of the bedroom, I walked by the main bathroom and stepped inside to tidy up what was left on the counter. While glancing down into the garbage can, there, neatly tucked away, presumably hidden by my husband, was a very long chunk of blonde hair, resembling the same colour of the hair on my daughter's head. I reached down to move the unused tissue to the side and pulled out exactly that. A chunk of my daughter's hair. To confirm my findings, I made my way to the family room with the hair, and asked, "Does anyone know whose hair this is?" My two kids and my husband looked at each other and started to laugh. My daughter, who was six at the time, had taken a pair of my old hair scissors from the bathroom drawer and cut the straightest line from her front fringe, one inch into the side of her hair, removing twelve inches in length. It was precise, and not noticeable until it was time to grow that piece out. One of my children cutting their own hair was bound to happen, and I just had to laugh, as I had done so many times before for other kids' curiosity adventures. Thankfully, my son never pulled this stunt, albeit, once the mushroom hairdo phase was over for him, he loved sporting a buzz cut, so a correction on his head would have been an easy fix had that ever presented itself.

Kids always get explanations from me as to why it isn't a good idea to cut their hair. This is partially to reassure the parent that I'm taking advantage of the teachable moment, and with any luck, it won't happen again. Nine times out of ten, the kids are embarrassed. I always let the kids know that I went to school to learn how to do what I do, and, "You cannot cut hair, especially your own hair unless you own a pair of real, hair cutting scissors. OK?" I usually get a nod of approval and understanding at this simple statement from the kids and a thumbs up from the parent.

Some children have physical and cognitive challenges that can add a layer of resistance to the entire haircutting experience. Some children don't talk at all during their haircut and others don't shut up. I personally love it when clients start to bring their little ones in for haircuts. Firstly, they grow into adults, and as I continue to work behind my chair, I can always use a new customer. Secondly, these spirited tiny people add so much colour to my daily routine, breaking the pattern of adult services. I don't really understand the decision hairstylists make when they refuse to service children, but we all must respect everybody's way of working in this industry. There is a place for all of us.

Salon personnel are aware that children can be demanding in a salon, particularly when it's time for their haircut and they are asked to sit still while we walk around them with scissors, razors, and other sharp objects that most of them have never seen before. Dubbing clippers as a "tickle machine" has worked miracles for me.

My very first client came into the hair salon located in a shopping mall with no appointment and was not partial to any hairstylist at the salon. At the time, I was a rising star hairstyling assistant for one of the owners. It was 6:00 pm and the owner came to me and said, "You have a client. It's for a perm and a haircut." I was in the back of the salon, folding towels when he startled me with this statement. I turned and said, "Wow! I don't have any tools here with me. I'm assisting you in the salon, remember?" I laughed. He didn't. "I'm going home for the day. Use my station and whatever you need will be there for you. Bring all your tools for your next shift. You're done assisting me." I guess I had just gotten a promotion, and this is the way the news was delivered to me… impromptu in the back of the salon, in the laundry room, right beside the restroom. This was my moment. Suddenly, I was done with mentorship guidance after only two months of being his sidekick and it was time to be the best hairstylist that I knew how to be. I didn't even have business cards to hand out to returning guests. Would this new client even remember my name? (This was long before cell phones and social media existed, so business cards were the way of advertising.) I went to the owner's station to set it up to my liking, searching the drawer of gadgets for what I thought I may need for this service. I then made my way to the front of the salon where my brand-new client was waiting for me. I introduced myself and we were on our way to a connection, one in fact that has lasted until today. She had two children, four and six years old at the time, and she advised me that both needed a haircut. Clients number two and three for me. My client base was growing substantially without effort, achieving a 200% growth rate in a matter of minutes. This was going to be a great choice in careers! I could feel it! Before leaving the salon, she booked upcoming appointments for herself and her children. I had been working for two hours and already had two more clients in the book waiting for my services. Saturday came quickly. When I walked into the salon, I unpacked my tools, set up my station for the first time and waited anxiously for my first request clients. It was quite thrilling to have a station to call my own, with my own tools. And before I knew it, my two little people arrived. The boy was my first client of the day, the second client in my career. He was a mild-mannered six-year-old, very polite, and on this day, not very talkative. His thick black hair wanted to stand on its own which was something that he liked, thank goodness. I finished his haircut with a little dab of gel, which made him puff out a little bit with pride and made him smile from ear to ear. He told his mom about the gel when he reunited with her, and of course, mom bought the gel on the way out from this appointment. Now, it was time for the four-year-old daughter. She grabbed my hand and held it all the way to my chair. Such a cutie! I helped her get up onto the booster seat and draped her with a towel and the same type of kid's cape that her brother wore. We talked about her hair, what kind of style she was interested in, even though she was getting a minor cut, the necessity to have gel in her hair just like her brother, and then, the questions began:

"Did you go to school to become a hairdresser?"

"Do you like what you do?"

"Are you married?"

"Do you have any kids?"

"How long have you been working here?"

"How much do your combs cost?"

"How much do your scissors cost?"

"Do you have to buy your own things?"

"Do you own this place?"

"How much money do you make?"

By this point, everyone working around me, as well as the salon guests, were listening in, likely to hear how I was going to answer all these questions, particularly the last one. There was no answer. I couldn't keep up with all her questions. To say that this little one spiced up the morning in the salon is an understatement. I knew at that moment that we would become long-term partners in the hair world, her as my client and me as her stylist, for as long as she would have me. Yes, these two little people are now adults, with children of their own, and, yes, we continue to see each other.

When I started to work independently, I got into a habit of giving suckers to kids after their haircuts and ended up making it a "thing" when I opened my own salon, supplying suckers for all stylists to hand out to their little guests, and the occasional adult that got wind of the perk. On one occasion, all ten stylists ran out of suckers at the same time and one of my clients had booked her son for a haircut on that day. No suckers to be had in the salon at any of the ten stations. We had even run out of candy and mints typically left in a basket on the front desk, which was another little something that was appreciated by clients. At the end of the haircut, I brushed off my tiny little man, removed the cape and towel from his neck and helped him down from the chair. He didn't move. He stood there staring up at me. He was waiting for his sucker, in his favourite colour no less, which always happened to be my favourite colour. I informed him of the very sad reality that there were no suckers to be had. I was not prepared for the utter meltdown that occurred. Neither were the others in the salon. "But I always get a sucker when I sit still!" Oh, dear Lord! His mother told me it was fine. It wasn't. I searched and I searched, but I did not find one sucker, not even the ones at the bottom of the barrel with no stick! My last search effort was in our staff room junk drawer. No sucker. I turned and saw my purse, and immediately rummaged through it to see if I had anything to eat in there that I could hand over to my distraught, little guy. In the end, he went home with a half-eaten roll of Lifesavers, an unopened granola bar that was most certainly put in my purse for one of my own kids, and a nearly empty container of Tic-Tacs. His mother laughed at the effort. I was in a sweat, and he was happier than a pig in mud for the time being. I was sure that he would remember this sad moment for a while. I felt horrible disappointing my tiny human with a failed tradition he had come to love, so I promised him a surprise on his next visit. A few months later, he was rewarded with a regular sucker, a colour of his choice, and I had also bought him the largest lollipop of many colours that I could find. He was made aware that this was a very special treat to make up for the last time he was in when I had no suckers. I didn't want him to think that this was the new "thing" for this salon. All was well and understood.

As my clientele grew over the years, the connections and friendships developed too, as life would have it, both with the parents and their little people. You see, the thing with kids is, they don't just walk into a salon by themselves. They don't have the means to get themselves there, nor do they likely have the money to pay for their services. So, dependent on their parents, they make their way to us, either because the establishment specializes in children's haircuts, or they are being brought to a salon that their parents frequent regularly. Hair salons are designed purposefully, housing expensive equipment, tools, sharp objects, and chemical supplies that certainly do not create a kid-friendly environment. Salon personnel find ways to adapt and accommodate families coming in so that everyone has a safe environment while receiving hair services.

One of the salons I worked in, in fact, one I had input in designing as a co-owner, was oddly shaped as an irregular quadrilateral. The front of the building was square and parallel to the busy front street, but from there, the entire building was shifted to the left, creating unusable corners at the back of the salon. We went with this because the building then took on the shape of the property and we thought that it would be an interesting design. As a result, our square washing machine and dryer didn't fit properly in the laundry room, a custom desk needed to be designed to accommodate the front waiting area, and there was dead space beside the hood dryers. Little people, my children included, had an uncanny way of finding these useless spaces and making them fun places to play, as these spots were all small enough for children to squeeze right in. The salon space and shampoo area were divided by two walls on either side of the space, creating an opening from one to the other, where three feet up, the walls were built to resemble steps making their way to the ceiling. Again, kids found creative ways to entertain themselves with this design. A friend of mine brought her three children in for haircuts one Saturday afternoon. As I cut the younger boy's hair, the twins hung like monkeys on either side of the half-walls shaped like stairs, which were right beside my station. With dirty shoes on either side of the walls, I could see scuff marks appearing on the white paint and out of the corner of my eye, I could also see my business partner starting to lose his cool. Mom, obviously used to chaos with these three, ignored her two hanging off the wall and watched her youngest get his haircut. I said nothing. She was my client, my friend, and a frazzled mom. Surely, I could remove the scuff marks after they left. Soon enough, it was time for the girl's haircut, where the younger boy replaced her hanging off the wall. Bookend behaviour amongst these children! Nothing more than a little bit of patience and some cleaner following this appointment was required.

Watching people go through fertility issues is a sad thing when you have been blessed with two amazing children. One of my clients suffered several miscarriages and I agonized every time. After many years, she was finally blessed with a beautiful baby boy. The child was born with a complete head of thick, brown hair, and to my amazement, she asked me if she could bring him in for a haircut when he was less than eight months old. I almost didn't believe her when she made the appointment, but I invited her to bring him in. What a surprise to see this little man with a full head of hair hanging in his eyes when he arrived. I got into a habit of giving complimentary first haircuts for my clients' children as these usually only required a few snips and it was over. I would place a clipping of hair in an envelope or stick it to a "First Hair Cut" certificate that I had made up for my mini guests, which included the date, time, name and age of the child, and the location of the salon. Under normal circumstances, this was a cute and effective souvenir for parents to do with what they wanted. This little guy's hair could have filled a large envelope or covered the entire certificate! I had never seen such a thing on an eight-month-old child. As he continued to come in for regular haircuts, at still such a young age, he refused to sit, so I would forego the towel and cape, let him walk and play with plastic clips or toys that his mom brought along, and chase him around the salon while I attempted giving him a symmetrical haircut. Often, he and I would both be sitting in the middle of the floor. This became the norm until he was two years old. There is a remarkable video online that features a barbershop with every stylist breaking out in song at the sound of a child crying in the chair. This act startles children into stillness so that their stylist can work quickly and give them their haircut. I could have used these talents many times in my career!

Always a challenge is a little cutie that comes in and requests to have hair "like my friend Sally" or "like my friend Jimmy." Hairstylists are a lot of things, but not mind readers, and if you don't have a picture of Sally or Jimmy, it's a crapshoot as to what the child really wants. Even the parents don't always know what Sally or Jimmy look like, and seeing the child describe these looks is often hilarious, and worth the extra five minutes that it takes to understand the request and oblige. Note to beginning hairstylists: the kid holding their hands up to above their ears to indicate where Sally's hair lands is not usually accurate. Do not, I repeat, DO NOT take the child's hair from the center of her back to the ears in one swoop. It is almost guaranteed that Sally's hair is not that short! Early on in my career, I found this out the hard way.

Denise Létienne

The era of the bowl cut in the early nineties developed one of my young humans into a creature of habit. He was a child of very few words, and to be honest, I don't believe that he liked coming to the salon, or me, for that matter. He had a thick head of hair with an undercut that he absolutely loved. The six-year-old would come in and request the same haircut as the order of the day. Every single time he was in my chair, he did not speak to me or his mother, other than his request as soon as he sat in the chair for his usual "same" type of haircut! He did not say "hello," answer any of my questions, or look at me. Typically, I do not like to repeat the same hairstyle over and over again. But here he was, for years on end, with the "same" order for his haircut, even if I suggested something different. Eventually, the bowl cut wasn't in anymore, at which point, it still took him a few years to let it go.

I am blessed with a four-year-old granddaughter and a twenty-month-old grandson. My granddaughter is very familiar with my home studio. She, along with her mom, dad and dog lived with us for a year when she was two years old. My salon space became another room in the house for her to play in, and never a scary place. On many occasions, she has been given a tripod with a life-size mannequin head to play with, along with a bowl half-full of conditioner and a brush for a messy "colour" application. I also supply her with a spray water bottle, combs, and a pair of gloves, so that she could mimic her Memère at work. She loves it in there! I do not take it upon myself to cut my grandkids' hair, as they are not my children, therefore I wait patiently for direction from their parents. My granddaughter has only had one haircut, taking a few inches off the bottom to even out her ends. She does often request to sit in the chair to get it combed or styled, albeit those moments are far and few between now that they are back in their own home. My grandson is blessed with exquisite curls on his very fine head of hair. Nothing is hanging in his eyes yet so I'm not sure when his first haircut will be. He does love to get his hair brushed though,

30

and with his language still developing, he will sometimes walk into the salon, will tap his head with his tiny fingers and look me straight in the eyes. When I ask him if he wants to brush his hair, a firm "ya" comes out of his mouth with the sweetest of smiles. These two are not afraid of my compact salon environment. They get to sit in the hydraulic chair when they want, and get a ride, either up and down or two spins around.

The reality of child clients is that they grow up to be adults… the adults who fill the pages in this book, the ones that have given me an appreciated and busy career since 1987. When teaching, I always encourage my learners to get to know the little ones. Little people sometimes create second and third generations of clients with one stylist. And if you're lucky enough, four generations.

I love my little people… the ones who have come and gone, the ones who have grown up, and the ones who have moved away. I am thankful for the ones who have blessed me with their presence in my chair, for the continued relationships that we shared as I watched them grow into adulthood, and for the gift of generations that continue to keep me lovingly working.

"The soul is healed by being with children." *Fyodor Dostoevsky*

Connections

There is an undeniable friendship that forms when someone hires you to be their "hair care-taker" and you take them on as a client. As people get to know us, discussions move past general chit-chat about hair and the weather. Before long, clients feel comfortable enough to have more serious conversations, get more personal and confide in us.

From the instructors that taught us in school to the platform artists that we watch at hair shows, we are always encouraged to stick to hair conversations during hair services. More specifically, we are taught to stay away from speaking about religion, politics or any other topic that involves strong opinions and controversy.

The reality is that when a client comes in every three to six weeks for a service, the "getting to know everything about your hair" becomes an uncomplicated task. It is our expertise. The hairstylist becomes more proficient in asking questions about "what is great" and "what isn't so great" about the cut, style or colour of their hair, and the consultation becomes smoother over time, more routine, and less time-consuming, as does the entire hair service. This does not mean that the client goes home with the same look for the next forty years of their life. New styles, ideas, and changes of colour reflect the change in times, trends, seasons, or events happening in the client's life. The service, from the time your guest walks in the door, until the time they leave with their new style, is always focused, including the best shampoo of their life, every single time that they are in the salon. In my opinion, if guests aren't moaning with delight at the shampoo bowl, you're doing it wrong! All this to say, once we get to know our guests, little by little, there is plenty of time to talk about many other things than hair.

It is possible, but most certainly not normal, to talk about hair for a two-hour appointment. Most conversations with my clients comprise of current events in their lives: happy times, stressful times, sad times, jobs, loss of jobs, new jobs, kid things, dog things, cat things, other pet things, current television show addictions, books, book clubs, reading in general, great authors, recommendations of movies, and health issues. The banter can be light and fun, such as pairing wine with certain foods, food recommendations, favourite restaurants, favourite sites to shop, both in-person and online, and favourite apps. We talk about so many things, mostly positive, at times negative. For the most part, I stick to the rules.

There is a trusting relationship that gets established with every client. In fact, there are not many professionals that have a license to physically touch their clients. It is common ground to get a handshake from a lawyer and an accountant, and depending on why you may be walking into a bank, you may get one there, too. But the professionals that really get to physically touch you are hairstylists, aestheticians, skin care professionals and massage therapists. Dentists, physio or athletic therapists, nurse practitioners, nurses, and doctors also have this licence to touch you. I may be failing to mention a few, but one thing that I know for sure is that the latter mentioned are people who typically do so with rubber gloves on for reasons… well, I'll leave the rest up to your imagination. For the record, I also wear rubber gloves, only to protect my eczema-ridden hands and save them from getting stained with colour. Other than personal services, are visits with these professionals always the most enjoyable visits? I remember rehabilitating a bad back from a car accident, and on another occasion, healing a broken ankle from sliding down a stair on my way to the laundry room. These rehab visits were exactly about the rehabilitation and were not the most pleasant of visits, yet necessary for my betterment. There certainly wasn't any small talk about my hair or about where I bought the shirt I was wearing. To this point, I hope that you understand what I am saying here. Touch! Physical touch! It is a profound gesture that connects humans. There is a trust that is required on the part of the client the second that they step into our salons and sit in our chairs. This trust allows us to touch their head, comprised of scalp, and hair, leading down to their shoulders, and occasionally, rub their ears to remove the colour from them. Salon guests are our lifelines. They are the absolute essential to our success. Without them, we are unable to have a viable business. And we recognize that! This is why it is so important to make them feel comfortable, especially because we touch them.

I have never professed to be the best stylist in the city. I do pride myself on the rapport that I have with all my guests though, and the way to do that is to behave as a professional and be kind. When my clients are in my chair, it is their hour, or two, or three. I am there to serve them and have always thought of myself as the person that was going to make them feel nothing else but great while they were spending their valuable time with me. Many in this profession have coined us "Day Makers." We are always happy to make someone's day!

For a very short time in my career, I serviced two guests at the same time. The process was to apply one colour, move the guest to a waiting area, apply a second colour on the next guest, move the guest to the waiting area, bring guest number one to the sink, rinse their colour, then move them back to the chair. Cut guest number one, bring guest number two to the sink, remove colour, guest number two sits and waits for me to finish guest number one. End the visit with guest number one, reunite with guest number two, and move back to the chair to complete. It was exhausting and I felt like I was cheating my guests somehow, where they momentarily lived as numbered people. I admire hairstylists that can work with future professionals while they apprentice in the trade, allowing the servicing of multiple clients in one block of time. It creates a very smooth system to accommodate the double-booking of clients, and the clients are always with someone who is taking care of them. That method of working was never for me. I was too greedy and wanted my clients all to myself. So, after I moved my salon to my home-based studio, I went back to what I call a relaxed working environment. I service one client at a time and I spoil them rotten while they are with me. One-on-one, quality time. I always have room for conversation, occasionally some treats and beverages that are sitting freshly made in my kitchen, and on rare occasions, sharing in a glass of wine. (Of course, this is for evening appointments only. I'm the last of the big drinkers and am pretty much done after one glass.) It gives us the time and space that we need to talk about hair, theirs and mine, and any other topic deemed to fill our space together.

We, as stylists, understand the vulnerability that it takes for a guest to share personal issues. The people in the lives of our guests present to us as "stick people" that we soon get to know through their words and stories. Unless they show us pictures of these characters, we don't know what they look like and likely wouldn't recognize them on the street if they were to be standing right beside us. We don't know them personally, and we will likely never meet them unless running into them by chance when out for a social event. I once had a client walk up to my husband in a mall and delivered a hardy "hello" to him, as she had seen his picture while in the salon. He had no clue who she was, yet, after she introduced herself, a short and friendly conversation ensued, along with a little bit of laughter at the situation.

Hairstylists organically become a sounding board, with two ears to listen, and a voice to respond when asked. Our listening caps are always on while hearing stories and we often take on the unauthorized role of a nurse, doctor, counsellor, and/or psychologist. Conversations sway back and forth from hair to personal stories, or recommendations to help correct various dilemmas. There have been countless articles, stories and books written about the relationship that exists between a guest and their stylist. It astounds some people how these relationships develop over the years. I sometimes get weird looks when informing friends that I am attending a client's wedding or funeral. This may give you a sense of what meaningful connections truly happen between a guest and a stylist.

The goal of the hairdresser is for guests to look and feel their best while in the salon and away from the salon. A fabulous hairstyle with the required product and tools to help them get on their merry way is our plan. And if it's a ponytail-kind-of-day, they need to have the tools and the know-how to make the best ponytail ever! It is important to me that my clients look and feel spectacular every single day, for the five weeks or so until we meet again for their next appointment.

It is inevitable. A trusting relationship between guest and hairstylist almost always turns into a friendship. I have clients whose entire families live out of town, so it is a fact that they visit with me more often than their own blood relatives. I have taken on clients at a young age and have watched them grow into young adults. This sometimes leads them into the dating game, creating lasting relationships, marriage, and children of their own. In between that, we sometimes hear of the breakups and witness the heartache. Having clients that are young and old presents many life scenarios that are talked about within the walls of the salon.

On rare occasions, we are privy to information that we'd rather not know. There was one odd time that a client came for a colour service and confessed to her stylist that she was having an affair with a married man. Yikes! There are no rules as to what the client wants to talk about during their time with us, and sometimes I guess, we are cheaper than a therapist and letting them say their piece is all right with us. The information can't go anywhere. We are bound by Freedom of Information and Protection of Privacy laws that prevent us from sharing anything. With no names mentioned, I will continue sharing some of this story, just so that you can get a taste of this situation, and how our professionalism kicked in to protect all involved. The client was elated, with a touch of guilt and shame, yet spoke loud enough for the entire salon to get wind of the story. The speaking volume in the salon rose rather quickly, as the other stylists attempted to drown out the potential of a gossip train that could have developed from her admission. The stylist did a fabulous job of toning down the conversation in her corner, and soon enough, the appointment was over. The stylist cleaned her station in preparation for her next client, unbeknownst to her, the wife of the man having the affair. Sweet Baby Jane! What was happening? A much different feel from the last client, and a reason why there is always a healthy supply of tissues nearby in the salon.

We hear a lot. Conversations are mostly good and fun, often about what the events for the upcoming week are, how the kids are doing in school, sports, or music, clients themselves taking on musical lessons as adults, or taking a path of healthy eating and physical fitness. We are privy to various medications that are being ingested for various illnesses or conditions, among other personal information. We are a safe place for people to dump whatever is on their minds. They share information or challenges that they don't feel like discussing with family or friends, like situations about their family and friends. It is sometimes a challenge to stay neutral. It's hard to contain ourselves and not to burst out and ask, "What the heck is she /he doing?" "What the heck are you doing?" "How are you allowing that behaviour?" "Are you sure that this is the direction you want to take?" What is allowed in these conversations is, "Hang in there, things will get better." "You are doing great!" "This moment too shall pass." and, "You are enough."

After having been in the industry for thirty-five years and counting, I really do consider the people that sit in my chair to be my friends. When I moved my salon studio into my home ten years ago, I trimmed down my clientele by hand-picking whom I wanted to have in my home. It was a small number that quickly grew again within a few months, which I allowed. Some people hand-picked me and refused to move on to the stylists that I lovingly recommended for them, and they were all welcomed back. There are a few whom I have formed stronger relationships with over the years, as they allowed me deeper into their lives, and I have allowed them deeper into mine. I have ventured out a little more with some and taken relationships outside of the salon where we don't even talk about hair, sharing paint nights or movie nights, and occasional dinners at our favourite restaurants. Having lunch at my favourite bookstore café with a client whose husband had recently passed away, sharing great conversation and a half litre of wine, was a very natural and enjoyable moment. Recruiting a client at my kids' hot-lunch program years ago resulted in her two daughters becoming new babysitters for my children and a friendship that I hold much value. My son's T-ball game twenty-eight years ago has resulted in a friend for life. Our sons were on the same team together, and fast-forwarding to today, our children (her daughter and my son) are now building a home together and planning a future. Yes, we are the ones who introduced them to each other seven years ago during one of her hair appointments when swiping left and right on a dating app wasn't working for either of them.

I have been invited to weddings and helped with recommendations for wedding venues and meal plans, funeral locations and eulogy wording, daycare programs and children's schools, dance and music lessons and their locations. I let my clients know that I can give them an answer, not necessarily the right answer when asked for advice. I have had a spouse come in to talk to me about his wife's mental health challenges to see if I could help at her next appointment. I've had flowers delivered to me on my birthday, coffee and tea brought to me during an appointment, ornaments and gifts given to me at Christmas time, and presents given to me for my grandchildren when they were born from people who have never even met my children. It is humbling to know how clients value you as their hairstylist and friend. They bring so much happiness into my life, and I hope I do the same in theirs.

Rarely, there has been cause to de-hire a client. This has not happened to me often, thank goodness, though I had to do it years ago. This was a client I inherited from another one of the staff, as they were not getting along anymore for reasons that I never cared to investigate. In retrospect, maybe I should have because after she jumped ship into my chair, it was two years of awkwardness. I was constantly reminded that I didn't know how to cut her hair, or apparently, dry it. She told me that she went home from the salon to re-wash her hair and blow-dry it after every appointment because I didn't know what I was doing. She kept coming back. According to her, her colour was always a shade off what she requested or was expecting. Our relationship ended with me in tears in the staff room at the beginning of her appointment as she told me that the last five weeks of her life were hell because she hated her hair. Strong words. You'd think that I would have thrown her out right there, but no. I endured another two hours of punishment with "Miss Negative." When I escorted her to the front desk at the end of her appointment, the first thing that I always did was book the next appointment, but this time, I went straight to the cash register (no computer back then). My words were something to this effect: "Listen, you clearly don't like anything that I do with your hair. I am out of ideas, and I have no more colour in my colour bar. It's time for you to move on to another stylist." Her reaction was slightly shocking. Her eyes welled up with tears and she asked, "Well is there someone here that can take me?" By now, all stylists in the salon knew her behaviour and no one was interested. "Everyone already has a full book, so, unfortunately, you will need to find another salon," I stated. She paid for her service and left the salon. Four weeks later, my salon manager came to let me know that she had booked another appointment with me. The day before her appointment, I cowardly got my manager to call her, and tell her that I was sick. I wasn't, but the appointment was cancelled, and she was not allowed to book another one with anyone else in the salon. I hadn't seen her since. Except, funny thing, last year I made my way to a grocery store I seldom visit and saw her walking the aisles. I never walked so fast in my life to buy what I needed and got myself out of the store before she spotted me. I had to take some calming breaths in my car before I drove away, which wasn't calming at all, as my head was rotating like an owl to make sure that she didn't follow me out of the store. It's a crazy thing how I allowed space for those feelings. Trust me when I say that this was a triggered moment. I'll work on not allowing that negative energy into my life ever again.

A nauseating experience from behind the chair happened in 2006 when my mother was near the end of her life. Awaiting the inevitable, I cancelled my week, rescheduling my clients or putting them in the caring hands of my salon team that rallied around me. When I came back to work the following week after my mother's passing, I found a stack of sympathy cards that had been dropped off personally or mailed to the salon from my fabulous clients.

They were all so amazing and compassionate, except for one. She came in on a Thursday evening and announced "I attended my daughter's bridal shower with ugly hair thanks to you." I was horrified. I looked her in the eyes and said very poignantly "my mom died." No reply. I'm not sure why I didn't escort her to the door of the salon that very night immediately after those shocking words came out of her mouth. I even had her back to do her hair for the dang wedding! She complained to me on her next visit that I had made her look like Debbie Reynolds and she didn't like any of the pictures that she was in. That was it. Adios! There is no need for disrespect on any level in this industry. Other than the two incidents noted above, I must say that I have been blessed with a wonderful clientele that I wouldn't trade for anything.

I was fifty-two when I made the move to my home salon and wasn't sure how long I would continue actively working as a hairstylist. I told myself that I would retire when my towels started to fall apart, though I have bought a few dozen packages several times since. I then added the mechanics of my chair hydraulics. If they give away, I will retire. I am thankful that great chairs have longevity, and I can't see them failing me anytime soon. My sink hose sprung a leak a few years ago, which was also a marker, though I chose to purchase two replacements rather than close shop. It turns out that my home salon set-up is convenient, gets me dressed every morning, and is one I'm not prepared to give up yet. I feel that health permitting, I will continue to work the hours that I do, trim them down when I feel the need, or quit should we sell this house. Maybe. There is always the possibility of building another studio in a different house. Don't ask me when retirement will be. I feel like I'm going to be one of those ninety-year-old stylists that can't put her scissors down. If no one is getting hurt, why not?

This career has been a gift. I have had the honour to meet many different personalities, each with a story of their own. All my clients are my favourites, yet I'd like to honourably mention the parents of one of my clients, whom I was lucky to know for a short while. Into their 80s when I met them, Mrs. G. would walk Mr. G. to my chair for his haircut, and before she left his side, she would tell me, "He is as handsome as the day he was when I met him." Then, she would kiss his balding head and slowly walk back to the front of the salon to wait her turn. Theirs was a storybook romance. Many years ago, a lovely young woman, Mrs. G. was out for a skate with friends, when she dropped one of her gloves as she was circling the ice. A very handsome young man who was skating by at the time, stopped, bent down to retrieve the glove, and handed it back to her. The courtship that started on that winter day formed a magical and enchanting seventy-year plus marriage. They were the sweetest couple that I have ever met.

It is not uncommon for a client to walk into the salon and greet us with a, "Hello, how have you been?" hug. It is also not unusual to end the visit with a "see you later" hug. Yes, we often graduate to hugging. How do clients become our friends? Hugs, I guess.

In 2017, after having lost two of my most cherished souls, I took to writing my homage to both on their online tribute walls attached to their obituaries. One read as follows:

My profession is a special one, and I LOVE it! I am not even sure that I can explain the impact that we sometimes have on our clients or the impact that they have on us. When somebody new comes into your salon for a service, they give you their trust in your ability to give the best shampoo on earth, to help them feel welcome and relaxed, and sometimes transform their inner spirit into their new self. We have a license to touch, and if you are lucky enough, a friendship is born, and a time in life is shared. My dearest friend... you had an appointment with me this coming Thursday! I will miss your presence in my home SO much, as you and I have shared many stories over the years. Dearest family, she was so proud of each and every one of you... she spoke so highly of all of you, every time we had our visits! RIP, my beautiful friend! My heart is broken.

This may give you a sense of what connections truly happen between a guest and a stylist. Connections. Respectful energy exchange between two people.

"A friend may be waiting behind a stranger's face." *Maya Angelou*

In Health and in Sickness

I take every single teachable moment to explain to learners how to handle difficult situations with clients, discuss how things were handled in the classroom, and what could have been done differently. One thing that is sometimes missed in hair schools is teaching future professionals how to cope with awkward, difficult, and sometimes strenuous situations. There are all types of clients, which often necessitates the need for those difficult conversations. This may very well be because these situations don't always arise in the time that the learner is in the school, or the teacher handles the sensitive situation with the one student involved with the client, as opposed to sharing with the entire class. Clients with scalp and hair diseases and disorders, or illnesses, don't always show up in the schools to give opportunity for the lesson. Adding a unit of learning in schools in this regard would make me happy. How to handle various situations in dealing with clients is not something that was part of the curriculum when I was in school. As a matter of fact, it gives me great pleasure when asked to go into schools as a guest speaker to share the business side with graduating students, which includes proper communication with clients on many levels. How to deal with, and service every type of client, and leave them feeling as though they've been treated with dignity and grace is one of the most important lessons a hairstylist can learn.

Over the years, I have learned that head lice, which is more common than you might think in daycares and schools, is not my favourite thing to deal with, therefore, I don't. As a matter a fact, some wonderful people saw an opportunity and a need for this service and have invested in mobile services to tend to lice-infested families in their homes. It's genius! This keeps all salon owners happy for not having to deal with the repercussions of bugs coming into the salon, and the subsequent need to implement necessary and proper sanitation protocols from such an event.

I have learned to care for plaque psoriasis for a client who is also riddled with a form of arthritis that prevents her from shampooing her hair and scalp in a way that can keep her psoriasis under control. She finds it challenging to apply her prescribed medication, and has discovered that a great scalp massage by me, with professional products, is a better solution. For this reason, she has a standing appointment to have her much-needed weekly massage and treatment with nourishing oils.

I have helped many clients walk from the front of the salon to the sink chairs and back to my hydraulic chair, who are either recovering from injury or surgeries or living with debilitating diseases that affect their mobility. I have learned to properly transfer frail bodies from their wheelchairs to the sink chair, and back to the wheelchair for haircuts and colour services.

I have run around the shop while cutting uncontrollable kids living with autism or kept them busy with song and dance while mom or dad served them a healthy portion of jellybeans to distract from the moving scissors. It helps to have a little bit of an "acting bug" living in my soul.

All of this, not taught or in the job description, quickly becomes part of the job if you love it enough. The more you care for your clients, the harder the job becomes. It is difficult to hear about these challenging times that your clients are living through, and you often inherently become part of the emotion, preparation, maintenance, and healing. Hearing a client share a cancer diagnosis is always a hard pill to swallow. One of my favourite things to do is to welcome a client back to the salon after a difficult and typically lengthy time dealing with an illness and treatment. That first haircut after illness is always a blessing for so many reasons. Survival is the main one. I have struggled to hold back tears when a client announces a cancer diagnosis, and hesitate in answering the question, "what would you do?" or "have you heard of this before?" I am more comfortable keeping my hairstylist cap on and sharing all information relating to hair and scalp that I have learned through experience behind the chair. I have learned that chemotherapy is a "cocktail" mixed and tailored to specific cancers, and different treatments have different effects on the hair and scalp. I have learned that shaving the head is, psychologically, a much more graceful way to lose your hair, than to watch it fall out and collect the clumps to be thrown in your bathroom garbage can. I have learned that the scalp becomes cold when you are used to having hair on it, and the sensitivity is sometimes unbearable as your hair follicles are affected by the treatment.

In the last four years of my career, I have lost one client to a heart ailment and two clients to cancer. The news of these deaths tore a piece from my heart each time. Staying in touch with these clients through email, phone calls and text messages during their fight, sending flowers, bringing the family meals in a time of need, and attending funerals is a painful process, as it most certainly is for the families themselves, living the nightmare. Conversations with clients while they are sitting in my chair sometimes include intimate details about family life. All the sharing about friends and family members over the years makes it almost eerie to attend their funerals or celebrations of life. It is sometimes easy to point out who is who, without ever having met any of their loved ones. It presents as a portfolio of their every being.

Once a client confides in a diagnosis, I always share everything that I know about the hair and scalp portion of their treatment. Finding out that they will lose their hair by their medical advisor is almost always as devastating as the actual cancer diagnosis. I make myself available, be it in the salon or during a home visit, to aid in the shaving of their heads. I do what I can to help people accept that their hair will fall out so that at least one part of their journey is an easier one.

I have taken women with long hair to a shorter style before shaving their heads entirely. I've had "shaving the head parties" (called that only to lighten the mood of the situation) either in the salon, most often after hours, or more often, at their home. Trust me when I say that these are not a party. Cancer becomes a family event, and often, kids, parents, spouses, friends, or other family members take part in the event in support of the diagnosis. The hardest one that I ever lived through was shaving my girl-friend Yvette's head, a friend of mine since the fourth grade, and a bad-ass breast cancer survivor! With permission, she is one of two names that will be mentioned in this chapter. I have never witnessed anyone who became so angry at a diagnosis before. She had absolutely no time in her life for cancer and was hell-bent on kicking this dreaded disease! When she told me the schedule of her chemo treatments, I gave her all the information that I had stored in my head and knew to be true about what was going to happen to her hair and follicles, and how we needed to handle it. She wasn't impressed. She was one of the ones I took gradually, from her long blond hair to a shorter style before her first treat-ment, while we waited for her hair follicles to let loose of her hair. She held out for as long as she could, not ever wanting to shave her head. In the meantime, I got hold of her wig, gave it some highlights, and cut it into a cute style, where no one would ever know that it wasn't her natural hair.

The call came in one Monday, early afternoon. I don't even remember her saying "hello", but I very poignantly heard, "I brushed my hair today and some hair started to fall out. Can you come over on the weekend to shave my head?" I paused and replied, "Your hair isn't going to wait until the weekend, my friend. Let's do this tomorrow night." She wasn't very receptive to the suggestion, but on Tuesday evening, I made my way to her house to find two vehicles that I wasn't familiar with parked in her driveway. Her son and her two nephews were waiting in the house, and two of them had decided to get their heads shaved in support of Yvette. The other nephew was there for support. They were already into the wine before I got there, so I joined in and had a few sips out of a small glass with them before I started the process. I had a little bit of fun in that kitchen that night before I started shaving her nephew's head. Yvette and I used to babysit him and his brothers when they were young. Yvette and I are the youngest in our families; there is a fifteen-year gap between me and my oldest sister and an eighteen-year gap between Yvette and her oldest sister. This gifted us both with nieces and nephews that are closer in age to us than our siblings. Witnessing this man, slightly younger than me, now a high school principal, supporting his aunt, gave me something to smile about during this emotional situation. The next person to get his head shaved was Yvette's eldest son. He was in his late teens, and very stoic as I removed the hair from his scalp with my clippers. Yvette told him a few times, "You don't have to do this if you don't want to bud," however this young adult followed through with his decision to shave his head in solidarity with his mom. Two down, one to go. As this wasn't my first "rodeo", I thought I was ready for the next step. I had walked into people's homes for their private "shave the head party" a few times already at this point. When it came time to drape Yvette with a towel and cape, I helped myself to a sip of wine as an overwhelming sensation came over me that hadn't arisen with other clients in this situation. This was a little too close to home for me to be a strong supporter. This was my long-time friend. The three guys in the room were watching me closely, and I could feel myself slowly fall apart. One of her nephews was standing right beside me, watching me attentively, and noticing that I was starting to falter. I positioned myself behind Yvette so that she could not see me wipe tears from my eyes. As I shaved her head bald, her nephew moved to stand behind me and hugged me tightly. I can't say that cutting hair while an adult man is hugging you from behind is common practice, but he could see that I needed assistance to get through and I needed both of my hands to do this task, otherwise, I'm sure that he would have just held my hand. His gesture was appreciated and needed at that moment. I worked hard not to be in front of her so that she couldn't see my struggle. When I did make it to her side, I saw that she too had tears. The silence in the room grew and remained that way until all her hair was on the floor. I used a soft dusting brush to remove the little bits of hair around her neck, removed the cape and towel, and when she stood from her seat, we hugged long and hard. Eventually, her two nephews and treasured son joined in. I had instructed the one hugging me to quickly pick up the hair and discard it before Yvette could get a look down at the floor and see it. When the long family hug finally ended, we both bent down to dispose of it. Everyone present that night was much-needed support, not only for Yvette but most certainly for me. Shaving the head of someone so near and dear to my heart is something I hope to only live through once. I don't care to be involved in such a personal experience again. I also know full well that there would be no hesitation on my part if I were called to this important task for one of my clients or friends again. God forbid. I'll be there.

Part of my learning how to handle cancer and its effects on the body and hair was with Audrey, an elegant client with a heart-warming soul. Audrey, a long-time guest, came into the salon for an appointment one day and announced in her usual happy and smiling demeanour, after her relaxing shampoo service, "I have good news and bad news. What do you want to hear first?" She looked so excited to be telling me what was about to come out of her mouth, that I in return, vivaciously said, "Always the good news first." "I have ovarian cancer, with six months to live" she proclaimed. "Jesus! What's the bad news?" I asked. "I'm going to lose all of my hair," she replied. In that very instant, it was confirmed that my job as a hairstylist was not always all about the hair.

Audrey fought long and hard for four years. I was with her every step of the way, as far as her hair was concerned. I sat down and wrote a short story a few months after her passing about the poignant moments that we shared in her journey. Writing has always been a coping mechanism for me, and something that I have always found to be therapeutic. It helps me process life situations and aids me in coming up with solutions to challenges that would otherwise remain inside my brain aimlessly without resolution.

"Audrey, a Pillbox Hat, and Me" was the title of the short story, written in the fall of 2000. Audrey was such an inspiration. She was a beautiful spirit who coloured her own hair, a lovely, "vanilla pudding" colour, I used to tease her. I could not convince her to let me colour it for her for the life of me, but she was so darned cute, that I was happy to be the one in charge of her haircuts. She was a strikingly beautiful looking lady, always put together from head to toe when she walked in the door and reminded me slightly of a younger version of my mother. One of her daughters, who was also a client of mine, and continues to be, wasn't as particular about her hair as her mother was. "Get on her to keep her hair in good shape" she used to tell me. Audrey had a lot to live for... three supportive children, six grandchildren, a wonderful husband, and a cottage at the lake, close to home, which was a family gathering place that she cherished. We shared a lot of stories during her illness. Her courage and strength were inspiring. She was a dream guest. I would greet her at the door, return her smile, and always ask her, "How is your body treating you today?" to which her response was always, "God gave me another day!" She lived across the street from the salon and always came to her appointments on foot, regardless of the weather. She talked to me as if I were one of her daughters, giving me advice on life situations, but only if I asked for it. She had many ups and downs in her last few years. I was involved in the purchase of her wigs and trimmed them as needed to make them just right for her. It took a lot of energy to hold back tears the first time that I shaved the thinning hair on her head. I would always offer to take her to the back room where it was a little more private, but she always declined and sat with her head held high, looking at herself in the mirror while clumps of hair fell to the floor.

Audrey had a love of angels. She came in for her Christmas haircut in December 1999, giving me a little magnetic notepad, which read, "Look for the angels in others." "It's for your fridge at home," she said. And there it lived. I loved that lady. The New Year brought new challenges for her. Chemotherapy was not working anymore and there was nothing left to do to keep her on this side of the world. She came in for another "shaving of the head" in the spring of 2000 because she was going to a wedding out east and wanted the wig to fit just right, so we gave it another trim too. That day, Audrey asked me where she could buy a little pillbox hat "like the ones monkeys wear!" she said. She was sick of wearing wigs and hats, so I told her that I would find one for her, and this became my mission. We both laughed and off she went. Until next time, my friend!

In May of 2000, five of my girlfriends and I went to West Edmonton Mall in Alberta for our 40th birthday weekend. We arrived on a Friday evening and made Saturday our shopping day together. When we stepped off the elevator in the mall adjacent to our hotel, I turned right instead of left and walked into a store that was so out of the way from everything else, you wouldn't go into it unless you knew it was there. My girlfriends told me that I was going the wrong way, but I kept on walking. There, at the front of the first store that I went into was a large A-framed wood shelf unit carrying hundreds of pillbox hats, just like the ones the monkeys wear. Coincidence? I was astounded at my find and stared at the colourful patterns of fabric that looked back at me. I chose my favourite and bought one for Audrey. I was so satisfied with my purchase that I could have probably gone home from that trip right then and there.

Upon my return, I called Audrey's daughter to ask her how her mom was doing. Not well, she informed me. Her daughter was coming in for a hair service that week, so she said we could talk more about it then. After her haircut, I gave her the hat that I had lovingly bought her mom and asked her to give it to her for me.

A few weeks later, Audrey called me and asked if I could clean up her hair because the "peach fuzz that's coming in is ugly!" "If you're feeling up to it, you can come in right now," I told her. It was a Tuesday morning, 9:00 a.m. and I had blocked time off to place a product order.

She walked in with help from her husband that day. It was the first time that he had driven her to an appointment with me, and the first time that I met him. She had lost a lot of weight and looked very frail. She was wearing that lovely and radiant smile of hers, a jean jumper with a white T-shirt underneath, flat shoes with socks to keep her feet warm and the pillbox hat. "Hello beautiful lady," I said. "Must be the hat," she replied.

My chair was the furthest away from the door, so I asked her if she wanted to sit at the one near the window. Her answer was no, so I helped her to my chair, trimmed her hair, and placed the pillbox hat back on her head. We slowly walked back to the front desk where her husband was waiting for her. "No charge, my dear," I said. She hugged me with all the strength she had left. As tears filled both of our eyes, she looked me straight in the eye and thanked me. She also told me "Be happy, be strong and love always."

Two weeks later, her daughter called me to let me know that Audrey had passed away on Thursday, July 6th, 2000. "My mom didn't want you to read it in the newspaper today," she said.

Relationships. Connections. Friendships. It's a hard thing when our "see you later" hugs with clients turn into "good-bye" hugs.

"I don't have to travel around the world to find my meaning." *Dr. Lew Losoncy*

My Days as a Hairdresser from Out of Town

I n the summer of 1995, my favourite distributorship sales consultant walked into our salon for his weekly appointment. He informed us that two manufacturers were looking for regional educators and asked if anyone at the salon was interested. It was a position that mainly kept you in the city and surrounding areas, educating fellow hairstylists on product knowledge and seasonal fashion trends in haircuts and styles. Typically, the job entailed visiting local salons and participating in regional hair shows, and offered ample opportunity to grow as an educator.

Our salon was already carrying one of the company's product lines and the other manufacturer was a new, up-and-coming company that was stepping foot into Canada after recently launching in the United States. One of the owners of this company was Canadian, which was of interest to me. Many times, my business partner and I had discussed having our name on bottles of products and it was a dream of mine to do so one day. My thinking was that this would be the epitome of owning a hair salon and having our own product line to enhance its success. We never did investigate the possibility any further and it never came to fruition.

We had a new hire in the salon and it was intriguing to watch her hone her skills. She was already very talented when she walked into our establishment and was a welcomed addition to the team. She was in her 20s with much to share in the world of hairstyling. I immediately thought of her to fill the regional educator position for the already-established company that was growing at an expediential rate. It didn't take any time at all for her application to be accepted and she immediately became an integral part of educating fellow hairstylists, and a valuable addition to their show team.

I decided to throw my hat in the ring for the new company, should they want me. To get hired, I needed to get to know the product, so I immediately ordered some stock for the salon that I could use on myself, my family, and a few guests. My business partner and I booked a class for our team with the Canadian owner on his next visit to town to promote his new line and educate those willing to learn about it. I fell in love with the product immediately and was looking forward to meeting the owner to know why I was feeling such a positive difference in hair when working with it.

After watching him work on the hair of two of my nieces who modelled for him that day, I confirmed in my mind that I was very interested in working with him. Throughout the day, as we got to know each other, he asked me to model for him for a "mini-show" that he was presenting that evening, hosted by the distributorship. This was a first for me. At that time, I was wearing my hair quite long and all one length in an era where clients were beginning to ask for the "Rachelle" cut, a haircut worn by Jennifer Aniston on the popular show Friends. The owner suggested that he would teach stylists how to do this haircut on stage that evening, on my head of hair, to which I agreed. With that, I was given a fresh colour to enhance the new look. Once the show was finished and everything was packed up, a few members of my salon team and I headed over to the lounge with the owner for a cocktail. At that time, I shared my desire to become an educator and he invited me to work with the company.

To finalize the offer, I needed to submit a video demonstrating my ability to speak about this new product. I discovered that it is easier to speak in front of a healthy crowd than it is in front of the red light of a camera held by your husband. After three hours of filming, I did make it through this five-minute assignment and submitted the video promptly. The owner called soon thereafter to extend a warm welcome to his team. What a thrill!

With the company being only months old, I was invited to a training session in Fargo, North Dakota with his team. Before I knew it, I was participating on stage at a subsequent hair show. This was the beginning of a fifteen-year relationship with this manufacturer. After the first day of training, I formed another friendship with a fellow Canadian team member who lived in Saskatoon, Saskatchewan, and to this day, she is a cherished friend. She lived in the same city as the owner and was by his side through much of his journey as he developed his career as a platform artist. She taught me everything I needed to know about working in front of an audience and behind the scenes of a hair show. We live 780 kilometres apart, an eight-hour drive, or a one-hour plane ride away from each other, and when we spend time together, we pick up just where we left off. She and I spent much time together travelling all over North America for training sessions and hair shows. We attended multiple awards dinners together in Toronto, where I had the honour of watching her win one year, always sharing hotel rooms, and catching up on each other's life.

Throughout this adventure, I worked my way up to becoming an International Platform Artist, which means that I was a hairdresser from out of town sharing product knowledge and other valuable information about this said company with fellow hairstylists. I taught and coached people on how to create the company's core haircuts and demonstrated fashion trends in seasonal hairstyles. One of my favourite things to do was motivational speaking, whereby I would guide licenced professionals to improve the way they operated their business, ultimately bettering their income. Sometimes my speeches would be geared toward guiding future professionals on whether they chose to work independently or under the management of others. Whatever their decision, I had a discourse on how to build their business into a successful career. The onus of getting busy as a hairstylist in the salon environment is ultimately on the stylist, not the salon at which you work, and I continue to share this important information in schools today when invited by my teaching peers.

I didn't travel the world working as an International Platform Artist, however, I did travel enough for me to meet gifted people from various locations in Canada and the United States who shared the same passion for our industry that I had. I attended multiple training sessions in my city of Winnipeg, Saskatoon, Las Vegas, San Francisco, Clearwater and Orlando, Minneapolis, and Fargo. Meeting talented people in each of these locations has provided me with a long list of acquaintances that I would not hesitate to contact today. And my spare bedroom is always most welcoming to them should they one day arrive in my "neck of the woods." The camaraderie in training sessions is stellar!

Hair shows took me to all the above locations, as well as Kelowna, Guelph, Thunder Bay and Toronto, and parts of the midwest in the USA. I have had many wonderful moments while working hair shows. I formed friendships with team members on several occasions, be it at breakfast, lunch or dinner shared, or at model calls, early morning prep times and evening downtimes. Meals are often provided to attendees, and the manufacturers' teams join and sit amongst them. This allows us to mingle with other travelling stylists, sometimes giving you a glimpse of your own industry mentors. I soon learned that no matter how famous and recognized the hairstylist is, people are people and want to enjoy a meal and togetherness just like the rest of us.

At one rather large hair show, when our team gathered at the table and took our first bites of food together, four people from a local salon came to talk to the owner of our company and began commenting to him how much they learned from our first day of stage presentations. The owner, obviously used to this kind of attention, continued chewing, covered his mouth with his napkin, and when finished with the bite of food, greeted the "fans" and shared a short conversation with them. The rest of us "newbies" on the other hand, dropped our forks and waited for the interaction to be finished before we continued to eat our now cooled-down meals. For me, it was a very tiny glimpse of a scaled-down paparazzi moment!

One of my favourite funny moments in travelling happened at a hair show where we were a team of eight, all working hard to put on the best stage show that we knew how. One of the hairstylists, already mic'd and ready for the stage, went for a quick bathroom break just before stepping foot on stage. Forgetting that the power pack was clipped onto the pants she was wearing, she pulled her pants down and down went the power pack into the still clean toilet! She retrieved the power pack and brought it to our technical support. When he opened the device, it leaked whatever amount of water it could hold onto the table and his pants. I'm not sure that he thought that it was as funny as the rest of us did, but I do remember still laughing by the time she made her way onto the platform. Comedy relief is always a good thing in a busy work setting.

I had the opportunity to see many fascinating things while travelling, and one most notably was seeing dolphins in the ocean in Clearwater Bay. This was not something I had ever witnessed growing up on the prairies in Canada. I was also amazed at the sight of the Rocky Mountains heading into British Columbia, though I had seen that from a train window once when I was very young. When in Florida in the month of February, a cold time of year for the Canadian prairies, I organized a five-day extension to my trip and was joined by my husband and our two children, who were six and eight years old, and we all went for our first visit to Disney World. What a treat!

Despite the educational rewards I received on these work trips, they were always busy and required extra stamina. One of my responsibilities was meeting with new distributorships and salons that carried our product. One partnership had me travelling to Guelph, Ontario repeatedly over the course of two years, where I took great pride and pleasure in mentoring distributorship sales consultants, salon owners and their staff. I enjoyed watching people grow to a deeper understanding of our products and become more successful in their businesses. The quaintness of the small towns surrounding Guelph had me awestruck. I often revelled in the beauty of 19th-century limestone architecture and enjoyed frequenting their pubs, cafés and restaurants, and the Elora Gorge, a stunning and popular tourist attraction.

In the spring of 2006, I was asked to take on the cumbersome task of delivering many classes in surrounding areas of Kansas and Nebraska because of a backlog of classes in the Midwest. It was originally scheduled to be a five-day trip, however, as the word got out that I was going to be in the area, I kept getting phone calls asking if I could add a day to the schedule. I ended up leaving on a Sunday and arriving home on a Tuesday evening, ten days later. After having organized the safety of my teenage kids at home, I left Winnipeg in the early afternoon with a short stopover scheduled for Minneapolis before landing in Kansas City. When I landed in Minneapolis, I made my way to a restaurant to pick up a light snack while I waited for my connecting flight. It was announced minutes later that the flight was delayed, and ultimately, was cancelled altogether at 10:30 pm. The airline automatically booked all the passengers on morning flights. I was assigned to a 10:00 am flight, thirty minutes after I was to be delivering my first class in Kansas. After making my way to the counter to retrieve my new itinerary, I pleaded my case to the reservation agent. I informed her that I had 200 people who would be waiting for me in a classroom the next morning and asked for a different option to get me there on time. A kind-hearted soul on my flight overheard my dilemma and offered to exchange her seat on the 7:00 am flight for mine. This meant cancelling both of our flights and rebooking them accordingly, and the airline agent informed both of us that there was a slight possibility of both seats being gone. There is nothing simple or guaranteed in the world of travel. With the help of another agent, the two, each on their computers, cancelled and re-booked both of our flights successfully.

After a sleep that could barely be described as sleep, I landed safely the next morning, minutes before the class was to begin. I was picked up at the airport by one of my team members, and of course, as luck would have it, I broke a wheel on one of my three suitcases in the process of running to her vehicle. The comedic relief was appreciated but not necessary. The participants were informed of my delay via email and were advised to attend the class one hour later than originally scheduled. When I finally reached the hotel where I would be living for the next two nights, I went directly to the location where I would be delivering my first class. When I walked into the hall full of attendees, the distributorship sales consultant, who had been getting minute-to-minute updates on my whereabouts, announced, "Elvis has entered the building!" Oh, my word! It made for an awkward situation, as I would soon be speaking to these people about work ethic and never showing up to the salon after your guest has already arrived. Being early was the name of the game! I laughed at my introduction, thanked everyone for their patience and asked them all to fill up their mugs and water glasses while I set up. With that, I was on my way to ten days of what was deemed "Denise's 'vacation' in Nebraska and Kansas."

Now known as a rock star, I delivered two to three workshops a day for designated salons in various areas, in both states, for ten days. Some events were larger than others, with attendees ranging from a staff of four to combined salon classes with as many as forty stylists at a time.

On day eight, it was, yet again, time to make our way to a new location. I must say, I could have done without this next incident. While travelling in a distributorship sales consultant's car on our way to Leavenworth, Kansas from Topeka for a morning session, we received a phone call from the sales consultant's wife, warning him of a tornado in our area. Before we knew it, we suddenly found ourselves in it! I had heard about the greenish tinted skies that could accompany tornados and was now witnessing it for the first time in my life. I could barely handle the stress of it all as I was death gripping the door handle of his car, which suddenly seemed to be an awfully small vehicle while travelling through this sudden storm. It appeared that we were alone on the interstate, passing overturned cars in the ditch and enormous metal highway signs that had been folded in half like paper by the force of the winds. At one point, we passed a semi-trailer that had been pushed over onto its side, with the metal sheeting of the trailer rolled up like a can of sardines. This may have been the moment that threw me into an absolute panic! We abruptly hit a stretch of road that was covered in large-sized hail balls, creating a road that was shimmying the car from side to side, as though we were driving on ball bearings. I had thankfully never witnessed anything like it before. At a time when built-in car phones didn't exist, the driver had long ago taken his wife off speaker mode and was now holding the phone in one of his hands while steering the car with the other. He clearly did not want me to hear what she was saying, and all I kept thinking was that he should have both hands on the darned steering wheel and maybe I should have been talking to his wife instead of him! I found out that there is no safe option when you find yourself caught in a car in a tornado. My suggestions of checking on the driver of the truck were quickly dismissed. I had visions of the movie Twister, waiting for a cow to come flying by at any moment, and cared nothing about participating any further, yet here we were! A storm chaser I will never be! We did survive the harrowing ordeal, and eventually, we were past the worst of the storm. We did, however, tag on an extra thirty minutes to what was supposed to be a one-hour journey. To me, it felt like hours.

Once we arrived, the salon staff were more than accommodating in allowing me a moment to compose myself from this extraordinary experience. While I was unpacking my tools, I was informed that I had just arrived in a cozy little city of thirty-some-odd-thousand that housed five penitentiaries. This day was looking up! Surviving not only the tornado but the entire ten-day education schedule took a lot of energy. Thank goodness for the support of my team and the local people helping me prepare, set up equipment, tear down displays, take me to restaurants to eat or pick up food, and drive me where necessary. Education is a well-oiled machine when you work for a great company.

Eventually, this company dissolved its partnership, leaving all its educators to decide whether to work for one partner or another or continue their separate paths. It felt like my parents were getting a divorce, so I chose not to continue with either of them, still loving and respecting both men who had taught me so much about this industry. One of them taught me how to build my business and understand the concepts of great hair and great service while successfully working behind my chair and operating a great salon. The other taught me a tremendous amount of science about hair and products that I never thought would be so important to understand my trade. His motto was "Science makes a better hairdresser" and he did everything in his power to teach us a whole lot about that. Working for this company gave me the itch to pursue teaching, and over the years, I obtained certification in Vocational and Adult Education and later, my Bachelor of Education. Teaching! Another one of my childhood dreams! Life is a giant classroom and life-long learning is a gift if you allow it. You can teach an old dog new tricks and I was happy to attain both certifications by the time I celebrated my 50th birthday.

I have never stopped attending classes or hair shows and feel that if I can learn one new thing from the experience, useful to me or not, then the investment in time and the price of the ticket is always worth it. Networking with peers is always a bonus to attending these events, especially since I have become a one-woman-show in my home. It's always a pleasure to run into old colleagues, students, and peers. I have had the opportunity to meet many of my industry mentors over the years. It is always interesting to see if they live up to the pedestal that I have placed them on. I have yet to be disappointed, as every single time that I have met one of these leaders, they have delivered more sincere kindness than I could ever imagine. In the last few years, I have participated in conferences at various locations in the Los Angeles area with a major manufacturer, meeting people that I have followed for years, both in industry and out. Owners of companies, celebrities from both television and the big screen, sports stars, spectacular people with important messages to deliver, now on missions to raise money in support of their designated causes and foundations, all humble and kind mortals.

There are many directions that one can take with a hairstyling license. In most parts of the world, hairstylists fall under the title of cosmetologist. This was so in Canada until the 1990s, when a division was made by our governing body, putting hairstylists into their own category. This separated the trades of cosmetologists, and nail and skin technicians. At that point, hairstylists no longer received in-depth education on skin and nails as I had during my training. A hairstyling license does not mean your only choice is to work in a salon. The education you receive can help you branch out as a fashion show stylist, editorial or advertising stylist, educator or instructor, stylist for film and theatre, or a celebrity personal stylist, educator for various manufacturers, artistic directors, salon owners and managers, or sales. Having a license does not mean that you need to own a salon to be successful. There is nothing wrong with sticking to servicing guests in the best possible way and owning the gift of your success in that position. Salon ownership adds a thick layer of responsibility and it is not for everyone.

And then, there is school ownership. In the year 2000, I found out a major hair product manufacturer based in the USA had plans to open a school division. There was an opportunity to collaborate with them, bringing a franchise or a partner school to our city. Their reputation is stellar, curriculum on point, and success rate a cut above the rest, which gave me huge hope for its success in our city. Trust me when I tell you that I did not give up on this one lightly! I had a plan in my head very early on and finally began working on a tangible business plan five years in when I could no longer keep track of the next steps. I began talks with the company and developed a relationship with them five years before finding a serious investor. I even made my way down to Los Angeles on numerous occasions for some intensive preliminary meetings and found out very quickly that it was an expensive endeavour. The chance to meet with my new business partner came when she was introduced to me through a mutual friend. Through relayed information, she and I met for coffee one day, which turned into a five-hour breakfast and lunch meeting. The next six years brought about forming a business relationship and friendship, travelling to the USA for information meetings, training sessions, spectacular conferences, and always stellar hospitality. We forged through on so many levels to get this project up and running, however, it was taking more time than I could ever have anticipated. As my 60th birthday approached, I met with my financial advisor, as I had done numerous times throughout these years, and I was forced to face the hard realization that investing in such a project was no longer conducive to what was next in my personal life. I was heartbroken at the reality of it all. Suffice it to say that this was one of the hardest industry break-ups that I ever had to live through. There were many tears on my part, and it took a lot of energy to stop the "what ifs" in my brain. They still live there, and I periodically get nudged of its possibility. I had to make an affirmative decision to walk away from this project, leaving my business partner behind. Although we no longer meet for coffee regularly, we do stay in touch, and I miss her beautiful and generous kindness in my everyday life tremendously. Even though this didn't work out for me, my advice to hairstylists, or anyone for that matter, is to take the risk on passion projects. The chance of success is there for everyone. This business partner gifted me with a distressed wood sign shortly after we met, and it lives on my dresser still today. The sign reads, "If it's still in your mind, it's worth taking the risk." I read this every morning of my life.

I see it as a privilege that I was able to experience the work involved in riding along with a manufacturer. I cherished every trip, even the one with the tornado, and was never overwhelmed by the work, possibly because I chose to keep my travel schedule small for the sake of my young family. As quoted by Chief Seattle, "Take only memories, leave only footprints." I hope that I was able to share my knowledge and help, even in the slightest of ways, with every stylist that I met in my travels as an educator. It was an honour to be part of this team and all that I experienced helped me with my growth in so many ways.

"Travelling – it leaves you speechless, then turns you into a storyteller." *Ibn Battuta*

Funny... and not so funny Things

With a career spanning thirty-five years and counting, I truly wish I had kept a diary of my life, especially one detailing the many moments I experienced behind my chair. When I got married in 1983, I purchased a journal to document a new beginning in a new life. It remained empty. When my children were born, I purchased a journal with hopes of jotting down moments of their young lives or funny comments that I hoped to share with them when they were adults. The pages remained blank. When I turned thirty, forty and fifty, I purchased journals to use as a tool for jotting down information and retrieving memories for the book that I always thought I was ready to write. They got tucked away in a box. I have a collection of them. When I turned sixty, I purchased another marvellous journal, with hopes of writing down wise words to share in the future or leaving behind a treasure for someone to read when I passed on to another life as my own mother did, or like the lead character did in the movie The Bridges of Madison County. My life isn't as juicy as the Madison County character, yet here I am, sharing some of my personal stories. I have purchased so many beautiful journals over the years, mostly because I have a weakness when it comes to pleasing paper products. Some of these new and unused journals have been given away as gifts over the years or used for other purposes. At some point, some were used to document events in my life and ended up being shredded… every single page, as some form of therapy, I guess, eliminating my past from my present.

Life in a hair salon is full of surprises on so many fronts. Good, bad, and ugly moments have happened to me while working at my designated station. There are some moments I'd rather tuck away and not revisit, some that are worth a mention, and some that are just too funny not to share.

If I asked any hairstylist in the world to share a story about something funny or traumatic that has happened while they were in the salon, I'm sure that it wouldn't take a lot of digging for them to come up with a story or two. Sometimes things happen during hair services that fail from lack of knowledge or experience, or other unforeseen situations. A hairstylist must categorize these events and put them in the "sh*t happens" pile for all kinds of reasons. There is no way of preparing for the out-of-ordinary situations that may present themselves, and quite often, the event has nothing to do with hair.

In 1987 while I was in school, there were two incidents that I experienced that took several learners out of the program. Yes, these events traumatized them enough to say, "This career isn't for me." The first incident happened to a fellow student, who, upon changing a blade out of her razor, pushed the end of a pen against the razor to release the blade. The blade came out abruptly, but milliseconds before that, her hand slipped with the blade coming down, cutting her arm in the worst of ways! This was by no means a safe practice procedure and had never been recommended. I had never seen so much blood from an injury, nor had I ever seen a person hit the floor so fast from losing consciousness. Paramedics were called, and because the school entrance was on a side street and on the second floor of an old building with a very lengthy set of stairs, I volunteered to go outside, wait for the ambulance to arrive, and direct them into the school.

I was two months pregnant at the time, and when I got outside, the fresh air and likely the shock of the whole incident almost knocked me into unconsciousness. I sat myself down on the concrete step with my head between my knees precisely when the ambulance arrived. The paramedics immediately jumped into action, taking my pulse, and began assessing who they thought was their patient! They almost didn't believe me when I told them that I wasn't the one they needed to be tending to, likely because my white skin was surely drained from all its blood, rendering me to a whiter shade of pale. One of the paramedics helped me back up the stairs, surely so that I didn't fall backwards on the way up, and so that I could lead them to where they needed to be.

We closed half of the clinic floor to give space to the paramedics and the girl in need. I took myself out of the mix by tending to our unnerved clients, who by then had been moved to the nail department. We offered them coffee and did our best to keep them calm. What a day!

It was necessary for the injured student to temporarily leave the program, as she required several surgeries to repair her veins and physical therapy to restore arm function and mobility. It was a pleasure to run into her at a hair show several years later. Her arm functionality was back to her new normal with some restraints, as she continued her path to become a hairstylist.

A few months later, another incident involved a woman who came to the school for a colour service. In the middle of her colour process, she began suffering a heart event, which truly is an event. I'm not sure why both incidents occurred right next to me when there were 150 people in the building, but there I was! We called 911, and once again, I volunteered to go downstairs to direct the paramedics up the long, concrete staircase. Incidentally, this time I was 7 months pregnant. The paramedics arrived and again, assumed that I was the patient, a woman in labour, or the one having the heart event! After more explanation, we went up the long flight of stairs and reached the guest who had been transferred from the hydraulic chair and placed on the floor with a slight cushion of towels placed under her head. The client was assessed by the paramedics and placed on the stretcher.

As they began to wheel her out, in a panic, I suggested that they allow us to remove the colour from her hair before taking her away in the ambulance. They looked a little puzzled at the request and informed us that this was a first for them. On a professional level, we felt that it needed to be done and they allowed the process to take place. We very quickly cleared out almost the entire shampoo area of the furniture to make room for the stretcher, shimmying her to a place where her head could hang over the sink to give her the fastest shampoo ever. Someone supported her neck as it hung well above the sink from the position of the stretcher and paramedics continued to monitor her while she continued her heart event. Once we wrapped her head in several towels to keep it somewhat warm, she was on her way to the nearest hospital, with an under-processed, uncut head of wet hair! Two days later, the school received a stunning floral arrangement, thanking us for the care of our guest, which was a sign of her having survived the day. Despite these two rather traumatic events, I became a licensed, professional hairstylist.

Working on mannequin heads is a fun and necessary process when learning the trade. At the time of learning, these heads seem to be the devil to work on, as most students would rather be working on breathing humans. The mannequins do help, however, in learning how to position the head while working and giving future professionals an understanding of how the hair falls with the use of our scissors, razors, and clippers. They also teach us that if heads are positioned properly, there should be no fear of cutting anyone's skin, anywhere on anybody's head... ever! Yet, on one occasion, low and behold, one of my jiggling little people did not keep his head still for one second during his entire service, resulting in an unintentional crooked haircut. His mother was harping on him, holding his head, bribing him, and nothing was working. I was doing everything I could, delivering some of my best dance moves possible to keep him somewhat immobilized while I trimmed around his ears. He was finally at a standstill, and at the exact moment that I was pressing my thumb to close my scissors near his ear, he did the fastest turn of his head, which ended up placing the tip of his ear in between the tip of my scissors! Yup! I did it! It's like when I catch a part of my knuckle with the blades and see it all happening in slow motion. You know that your skin is in between the blades of the scissors yet your brain continues to push the thumb hard enough to close the two of them together, which draws a healthy amount of blood at the bend of your finger. I did the same with this child's ear. It happened before I could stop it from happening. It wasn't a big gash, just enough to draw a little blood and render him stunned. His eyes were wide open, and he was staring at himself in the mirror, almost searching for a piece of flesh to fall! He did not move one inch until his haircut was complete, and for the remainder of the time in my chair, he stared at me through the mirror, as though I had cut his little ear on purpose as a ploy to have him stop moving. In those days, I always had a supply of styptic pens, which contain a white powdered substance that clots bleeding. A little bit of that healed everything and the visit was ended with five suckers versus the usual one.

There are times when I almost can't believe I have a clientele that willingly continues to come back to see me. I've hit so many people in the head with either a brush or the tip of my blow-dryer over the years, yet they continue to come back. I have also rescued many from failed self-haircuts, home colours, and previous stylists that they no longer jived with, so I guess my good outweighs my bad.

When I began working as a platform artist, the very first hair show that I was invited to participate in was in Fargo. A quick training event before the show, and then I was on! I had already worked backstage for the company, helped distribute product information and samples, ensured every chair was positioned to see the stage and greeted and welcomed fellow hairstylists to the show. But this! Heading up the stage with the front-liner was a first for me and quite exciting. I had things to share with my fellow industry professionals.

We hit the stage, lights on, microphones live, and the show was in progress. Having just learned the cutting system we were about to showcase, I realized halfway through that I didn't completely know what I was doing with this particular haircut. I started to have what seemed to be a hot flash, possibly because I was under very bright lights. There I was, for all to see, having what may have been a panic attack! I knew that I was doing it wrong with no idea of what direction to take from this point and couldn't see a way to stop the show to ask for instruction without making myself look like a fool. I managed to snap myself out of my brain cramp, unlearned what I had just learned, and quickly taught myself my version of this haircut in front of the 500 hairstylists in the room! Thankfully, this was at a time before cameras zoomed in on the action to catch every detail of what was happening on a projected big screen. Knowing that people sitting past the third row usually don't see the detail, I was able to calm myself down to end this demonstration with a little bit of class. My model gave me an unrehearsed hug as she left the stage. She loved her new look so much that after the show, she told me that if we were ever to come back to the area, she would be more than happy to model for me again. The owner of the company couldn't believe that I had gotten out of that presentation somewhat unscathed.

Four years into working for this company, I was honoured to be asked to support the team on the main stage event of our annual, local hair show. I was elated! We gathered top city models to be our live hair models for the show, with consultations and prep work held with them in my salon the day before the event. Our "opening act" model had her original lighter blond hair colour transformed to a rich, dark colour before the hair show. As the music started, the owner of the company walked out from backstage, went directly to centre stage where our model was sitting with a hooded cape, and in one dramatic process, he pulled off the hood, brushed 20 inches of her hair in one hand and cut it off while using a razor with the other, flinging the freshly cut hair behind him for everyone to see, but her! This was done for noticeable effect, of course, as the model already knew what was about to happen. Once her haircut and style were complete, she paraded down the stage runway after having removed the cape and dropped it to the floor, with a new pixie cut that garnered many comments, smiles and applause.

A few weeks after the event, this model contacted me to see if I could take her hair back to her lighter colour. When she arrived at the salon for her appointment, she had a picture of a similar haircut, quite blonde in colour, which she wanted me to replicate. This had me in a little bit of a panic. When we originally met her, she was already quite blonde, and the integrity of her hair was compromised from multiple processes before what was done for the show. This was the reason she allowed us to cut 20 inches of her hair in the first place, with the model agency's consent, of course. I decided to give her highlights instead of changing her hair colour completely.

In those days (we're talking late 1990s), we placed thick rubber caps on the heads of our clients and used a fine crochet hook to pull short hair through tiny, perforated holes, so that the colour change would happen to the hair sticking out of the holes. Even though I invested in these expensive caps in various sizes to accommodate all head sizes, it was my opinion that this process was never OK, but I did it anyway. After the first process, I concluded that the hair was not light enough and applied a second dose of lightener. I let the hair sit for the predetermined amount of time, keeping a close watch, and then, upon removing the cap, her freshly highlighted hair came off with the removal of the cap! Can you say, "Lost this client forever!?" Or so I thought. I gave her a detailed explanation of what had transpired, and I took her back to the darker chestnut colour that she adored. She continued to visit me in the salon for several years until she moved out of province... or did she? This is funny now, but it most certainly was not funny then. It has, however, given me a great teaching tool, which I still relay in classrooms today, even bringing the cap with me as "Exhibit A" to show the learners what kind of shenanigans I encountered throughout my career. If you stay in it long enough, you can gather some very interesting and funny stories.

My business partner thought that this incident was hilarious and decided to pull a practical joke on one of his clients who was getting a permanent wave at her next appointment. In the backroom, he took the time to retrieve some dark-coloured hair out of the trash, the same colour as his client, and wrapped a perm rod with the hair, even putting a little bit of the leftover perm solution on the prop. When the time came to unwrap the rods from his client's head, he pulled the "broken rod with hair" out of his pocket and showed her, telling her that her hair was breaking at the scalp. She looked stricken with shock! Thankfully, he couldn't keep a straight face for long, so the client didn't have a lot of time to process what was happening or get upset. Those were the days when we sometimes weren't so classy behind our chairs.

There was something in the air that spring, and one event from that time still has me shaking my head to this day. It could be categorized as strange, funny and divine, all at the same time. Funny after the fact, and divine because nobody was harmed in any way, shape, or form as it unfolded. Our salon was on a busy four-lane street with two lanes heading south, and two lanes heading north to downtown, divided by a median with trees spaced out every ten feet or so. Directly across the street from us was a small strip mall housing a credit union and a few other small shops. One Tuesday morning, a car pulled up in the parking lot by the credit union. As the driver hopped out of the car, she inadvertently shifted the vehicle into reverse. Oblivious to what had happened, she stepped out of the car and entered the credit union. The car was on a slightly slanted surface which was enough for it to stay put for thirty seconds but was also on enough of an incline for the car to start moving toward the street.

I was standing at the front desk waiting for my next guest and talking to my receptionist. As we looked out the window, we watched in horror as the car began to slowly slide out of the credit union parking lot, jump the curb, cross two lanes of traffic, jump the median between two trees, cross the next two lanes, jump the curb again, make its way into and across our parking lot, and slam into our building between two of our six windows! I yelled for everyone in the building to run to the back while I stayed closer to the front to see if the car was coming inside for a landing. The front wall, made of wood and stucco construction, caved slightly, thankfully stopping the car in its tracks. While the staff watched in horror, I ran outside, jumped in the car to shift the gear into "Park" and turn off the motor. When the owner finally came out of the credit union, she looked dumbfounded, and searched left and right to see where her vehicle had gone. I screamed, "It's over here." She was quite taken aback, to say the least, ran across the street to retrieve her car and asked us how it got there. She was completely surprised to find out that it had made its way into our building by itself. She apologized profusely for this unfortunate incident. The insurance company acted within an hour on this claim, as we needed to ensure that the structure of our building was safe and sound so that we could continue operating. The following Tuesday showed no disrepair to the salon. This incident certainly created a great topic of conversation about non-hair-related issues in our salon for months. It was amazing that not one vehicle on this busy street or one person was injured in this mishap.

The funniest, non-intentional incident that has ever happened with me in the salon, would make a hilarious skit on the set of Saturday Night Live. Or maybe not.

To this day, it is a rare thing for me to take a day off work because of illness. It would have to be something major, as rescheduling is often a nightmare for me and an inconvenience to my clients. On this particular day, I was at the tail end of a cold that seemed to never end. I had gone through all the usual symptoms… fever, chills, runny nose, cough, with the brunt of those short-lived symptoms occurring on my days off. I eventually got to the place where all seemed well, that place where you feel fine, you look fine, yet the hacking cough that has you gasping for air lingers.

On my first day back at work, I was worried that my cough would turn into unannounced coughing fits, with no end in sight once I start. The way to control this in the salon is to keep your throat from drying, by drinking copious amounts of tea or water and constantly sucking on throat lozenges.

As a stylist, I love to converse with my clients, but on this day, I told them, "I'll let you do the talking today." in anticipation that my throat would dry up, creating an unwanted bark. I was armed with a plethora of lozenges, in many different strengths and fla-vours that held the coughs at bay. I made it through an entire hour and a half of a client's colour service without one outburst. I was surely showing signs of being at the end of this six-week cough that didn't seem to want to leave my body. We had made our way back to my station for her haircut, where I settled her in with a fresh towel and cutting cape. I placed a fresh lozenge in my mouth and proceeded with the haircut. With no warning whatsoever, a coughing fit came out of nowhere. The abrupt cough caused my lozenge to shoot out of my mouth like a small cannon, where the lozenge landed directly on the centre of my client's head! I had no time to turn my head away or even cover my mouth before I realized that it was happening. She didn't move. I began hysterically laughing to the point of no return. Coughing, laughing, and crying, I could not contain myself! I made my way to the staffroom in the back of the salon to catch my breath, drink some water and stop the coughing, abandoning my guest in the process. A good ten minutes passed before I got myself back to her. She was sitting statue-like, in the same position I had left her, she had not moved one inch, and, unbeknownst to her, the throat lozenge lay on her head in the exact same spot. Her first words to me were, "What was that?" I started to laugh again and told her that I had coughed up a lozenge on her head. "I was wondering," she said calmly. We took a short trip to the sink to re-wash her hair so I could pick the "now stuck" lozenge out of her hair. I could not apologize enough for this incident. Thankfully, this was a good friend of mine, one I've known since childhood. To this day, we can laugh at this silly incident, along with so many more.

In any building, in any environment, and in any workplace, there is always an opportunity for funny (and not so funny) things to happen. I'll never forget the time that I had cleaned my station, packed up all my things, and was ready to walk out the door after a busy Saturday. There were a few of us gathered in the staff room at the time, and as I put my coat on and grabbed my purse and my briefcase, my business partner wished me a good weekend, left the staff room, only to turn around and come back in immediately. He looked me straight in the eyes and said, "Did you know you still have a client under the dryer?" We all burst out laughing! I quickly placed my things down, took my coat off, and made my way to my client, not sure exactly how long she had been sitting there reading her book. She hadn't melted and wasn't red in the face, so it couldn't have been that long. I brought her back to my station to finish up her service. She was none worse for wear, and nobody let on that I had forgotten about her. I was just thankful that they didn't have to call my house to get me to come back to the salon!

A hair salon offers a unique workspace that provides close contact between people of all ages for various lengths of time. Our space holds sharp objects, strange-looking chairs, hood dryers, orbiting infrared dryers, odd-shaped sinks, shelves full of products, and tools and equipment typically not found in any home. The size of the salon and an occupancy permit determines the number of people that one salon may hold at one time, including its staff members. Sometimes, that number exceeds the limit slightly, with parents bringing multiple little people in for hair appointments, caregivers accompanying the physically and cognitively challenged, entire bridal parties and their families, or friends coming in together for services to keep each other company. With more than one person in a room at one time, life unfolds as it does in our salons, and the interaction between one human and another creates many chances for these incidents to happen on many levels. I wouldn't trade this career, full of funny (and not so funny) things for anything.

"To make mistakes is human; to stumble is commonplace; to be able to laugh at yourself is maturity." *William Arthur Ward*

Women in Business, Endurance Required

I saw an excerpt of a Taylor Swift interview, filmed in August 2019, where she spoke quite frankly about the different vocabulary that exists in her business world. She gave the example of the following about the music industry: "When men do something, it is viewed as strategic. When women do the same thing, it is viewed as calculated. Men are allowed to react. Women can only over-react." Sadly, I must agree that this vocabulary exists in many worlds, where men and women are in the same field of business yet are often treated differently in a variety of circumstances because of their gender. This also exists in the hairstyling world although, in my experience, to a lesser degree.

When I was younger, I worked at various jobs including as a junior employee at a fast-food chain, in the kitchen of a prominent hospital, and at a large, highly regarded insurance company. I then joined the hair world, and two years into attaining my licence, I went into a partnership arrangement with another hairstylist and

79

owned my own business. In all these places of employment, I recognized that the treatment of women in business, on many fronts, was unfair, to say the least.

In the creepy old building of the fast-food chain where I worked in the downtown area, the change rooms were in the dungeon-like basement, along with a storage area and the managers' offices. It was a horrible design. It took just one time, while changing in the dark and damp change room, that a sexual comment by one of the managers shifted my routine to arriving to work already dressed in uniform and leaving the same way, even if I was covered in grease from french-fry duty. "Changing in the open would have been a better thing to do so that I could get a better look at your beauty." were his exact words. The derogatory comments and advances also came inside the walk-in fridges, in the back area where burgers were being assembled and in the well-hidden corner where the food packaging was kept. That gig didn't last long. Three months was my limit. At the age of sixteen, I wasn't equipped with the tools to walk out after the first incident. I was taught to commit to responsibility, and although I knew that the comments were inappropriate, I also believed that walking out after signing a contract was irresponsible. When I did decide I'd had enough, my father was thrilled about me leaving that place, mostly because it was in the downtown area, and I was bussing to and from work at odd hours. He was never made aware of what I endured there.

From that job, I interviewed for an entry-level position at a hospital, working in the kitchen as a 'tray loader.' I was loading trays of food into carts to be taken up to the wards for patients. My shift began at 4:15 pm each day and we promptly began to assemble prepared dinners for the sick. No sooner did we get all the trays loaded and on their way to the patients, did they start coming down, back to the kitchen, eaten and cleaned of food, or partially eaten. Some trays would come back untouched because patients were either too ill to eat or may have been discharged and that bit of information hadn't reached the kitchen in time. When we finished placing food on trays, I would move from the food side of the kitchen to the dishwashing side, where I would again place myself at the front of the conveyer belt and load the now dirty trays onto the belt, for people to unload whatever object was their assigned task. There were cutlery people, bowl people, large plate people, small plate people: the synchrony of it all was amazing to watch. At the end of the conveyer belt, was a large, wall-sized industrial dishwasher, loaded by yet another person, and one at the other end, removing the freshly washed items and stacking them for the next meal. Most of the staff in the kitchen were female, with a few males doing the heavy lifting required. I'm not sure if it was because of the hospital's "catholic" environment (it was run by nuns), but I never witnessed any wrongdoings as far as advancements or harassment toward women were concerned. At that time, gender-assigned duties were certainly in place, and it was generally accepted that males made a bit more per hour than females. "Why was that accepted?" is the question I ask myself now.

I met and began dating an orderly from that hospital a few months before my grade twelve graduation. We connected when a co-worker was ill one day, and I was asked to replace her on elevator duty rather than tray loading. Not knowing exactly how to work the antique elevator with the manual handle, I got myself stuck for a period of almost two hours, along with two carts full of food. Thankfully, I had already dropped off the third which gave me room to sit on the floor waiting to be saved. Of course, this caused a major reorganization by the kitchen staff to get food to the patients. Luckily, the elevator had a direct phone line to the kitchen, so I was able to inform them which wards had food in the elevator with me. These trays of food all needed to be re-filled and delivered from an adjacent elevator across the hall from the kitchen. Oh boy! The food was starting to smell rancid by the time

I was rescued by the maintenance crew. They had to hoist me up to safety and freedom as I was stuck between two floors. Having helped myself to a few too many cookies, juice and tea from the patients' trays, I was starting to feel queasy. The orderly was there to help rescue me, and before we knew it, we began our young, three-month-long courtship. Suffice it to say the kitchen didn't ask me too often to replace in that position. I worked happily at that hospital for two and half years, nearly incident-free. I am glad to say that in today's world, here in Manitoba, all positions in both medical and teaching fields are compensated based on position and experience, and no longer based on gender. Both large sectors are guided by the provincial government, which keeps the playing field fair, and equality is a non-issue. Sadly, clients of mine still deal with and endure discrimination because of their gender, religion, or colour of skin. That is not allowed in my salon or my home for that matter. I also feel that I am not qualified to speak more on this subject, as the things that I experienced working as a white woman are all that I know, which is nothing compared to what visible minorities must endure.

My first permanent, full-time position was at a large and reputable insurance company. At the time that I was hired in January 1979, there was a DJ at a local radio station who let it be known, particularly when the weather was warm, that he was going to sit in the park across the main doors of the insurance company to watch the women of the said company walk in and out of the building at lunchtime. He was always commenting on how so many attractive women in the city worked at this company, and this seemed to be all right with everyone. No one ever complained or commented on his words. He was never reprimanded or released from his duties as a DJ from the radio station for what he was saying on air. To all, including me, it seemed this was perfectly normal and acceptable behaviour. As a matter a fact, when I got hired, I was happy to be part of the group of women that worked there for this reason, as though beauty was a condition of employment. The hire gave me an unhealthy acceptance of my appearance, and in my mind, categorized me into a league that I never once thought of before working there. Every morning, I would listen to this radio station and drive in proudly, with the feeling that I was being personally talked about by the announcer for the entire city to hear. Good gravy! The objectification of it all!

Because I was fluent in French and English, both official languages of Canada, I moved up the ranks rather quickly at this international company, as we supported branches across Canada and the United States. My final position after nine and a half years of working there, was in a department that was divided into three sections, with three supervisors, one for each sub-department, and one manager. I was the supervisor for my section with three women under my wing. The remaining twelve employees were men. In my final year, there was a substantial change being made to the company's computer system and we were told to prepare for a potential disruption in service with a need to support our users. We knew this would affect the day-to-day business of every office in North America and our clients were forewarned of the potential disruption. Without warning, the outages began earlier than expected and phone calls quickly began flooding my department. The disruptions were causing much confusion and unreasonable delays for our clients. A late afternoon meeting with the three supervisors and the manager was called to discuss the situation. Concerned about the lack of customer service, I asked a question about the continued process of the upgrade. One of the supervisors promptly and unfairly shared with the group that I was incompetent and, in his words, should read the memos to understand my job better. He also called me a few choice names, some that started with an adjective, a four-letter, "f" word, and not words like fair, or fool, which would have been easier to swallow, but a rude word to accompany the poignancy of his message to me in front of my peers. After his rant, he took it upon himself to make other disparaging comments to me about having requested this meeting and wasting everybody's time. He exited the room, leaving the other three men and me dumbfounded, slamming the door behind him. The meeting was abruptly adjourned. Nothing further was discussed. Nothing was said about the supervisor's outburst. Nothing was done after the fact. Nothing. Rien. Nada. Even after a trip to my manager's office to request an apology at the very least, I was told that this was just the way it was, this was the way he was, and I was told to let it go and go about my business. The incident was laughed at in the department, though a few kind co-workers apologized for the behaviour of their peers. It was never their job to apologize for someone else's behaviour, yet their support gave me some comfort and allowed me the dignity to continue walking through the doors every morning, for a little while at least. This incident created a toxic work environment for me and caused me much stress. It led to more than a few trips to the doctor, as I began to have stomach issues and started to lose weight at a time when I did not need to lose a pound. I quit working there nine months later. My health was being compromised for no good reason, and after much medical testing, the conclusion was that I was under duress. There was a huge sense of relief and peace of mind when I left the corporate world to start my education in hairstyling. Finding out that "the guy" had contributed to my going-away present, and added a "good riddance" to his contribution, made me cringe. For the most part, working for this company was a happy chapter in my life, yet I was so relieved to leave it behind.

There seems to be a degrading attitude toward hairstylists and the beauty industry in general. When I quit this job, I went to the local bank to close my accounts, which was situated at the end of one of the hallways of the company. The teller, whom I had been dealing with for almost ten years and had become one of my favourites, asked where I was moving. I informed him that I was not moving per se, just leaving this job to pursue a career in hair-styling. I wish that I could have taken a picture of the expression on his face as he asked me, "Why?" followed by, "Your hair always looks great!" His response made me feel as though I was leaving all my brains behind to take on an inadequate career choice. I've never understood this school of thought. It may stem from the olden days when young women got pregnant and were sent to Beauty School, which at that time, coincided with the nine-month-long course. This is a fact, believe it or not.

Six years after attaining my hairstyling license, and five years after ownership of my eight-station salon, it was time to grow our business. My business partner and I purchased a property and constructed our very own building to house a bigger workspace. We found the perfect location just a few blocks away, where an old, dilapidated farmhouse sat as an eyesore in the neighbour-hood. We purchased the property and hired a private contractor to manage the build of our new, 2000 square foot salon, not overly large, yet a substantial upgrade from our 850 square foot rental. Before making an offer on the property, we needed to get our finances in order. At the time, we were dealing with a large bank that had a commercial division. My male business partner and I scheduled an appointment with our branch manager to talk about getting a mortgage for our new endeavour. I spent weeks prepar-ing a business and financial plan, along with updated resumés for both of us, and a summary of our net worth. I printed four copies of each and placed them in separate portfolios for our meeting with the bank manager, with one to spare in case another bank personnel would join in the meeting. On the day of our appoint-ment, we were greeted at the door upon arrival and escorted into the manager's corner office. Impressive, as it only took ten seconds to get to the manager from the time we walked in the door. The manager stood at his office door waiting for us, where he intro-duced himself to my male business partner with an extended arm and a hardy handshake. The manager ignored me completely and made his way back to the chair behind his desk. "Have a seat," he said, and then, "Are you two married?" It was a question that we got a lot, to which both of us laughed and replied that we were not, to each other in any case. I pulled out the portfolios, but before I could distribute the finely prepared packages, the manager proclaimed, "You don't have enough money in the bank to do what you want to do. I don't want to waste your time or mine, so I suggest that you abandon ship with your plans to expand your business at this time." I had one failed attempt at getting him to look at our business plan. One failed attempt in discussing the process we needed to follow to get this project done. One failed attempt at getting some banking information from a person who did not do his job that day the way that I needed him to do it to help us move forward. The meeting was over, in his mind, before we arrived. We stood up from our chairs, leaving the bank feeling like young children who had just been scolded, but not without me first, walking closer to him, extending my hand, and giving him a handshake upon leaving, while saying, "I'm Denise. Thank you for this experience." When my husband got home from work that day, he was made aware of what had transpired in my meeting. The next day, we made our way to the bank to pull out every single penny that we had in retirement funds, mutual funds, savings accounts, checking accounts, and thankfully, our mortgage was up for renewal within a few months of this incident, so that came out as well. We were a young couple with two young children and it likely wasn't our money that was making this bank thrive, but it was our pleasure to make a statement. What a terrible and humiliating experience! To this point, not all banks and managers are of this nature. One of the hairstylists working for us at the time conveniently had a father managing the commercial branch of a different bank and suggested we go meet with him. He was kind-hearted and spent ninety minutes with us, directing us on how to make this proposition feasible. My business partner and I did not abandon ship with our plans to build our new salon. As a matter a fact, with the help of a wise and generous father-in-law and a non-chauvinistic male bank manager at a commercial business development bank, we were guided to success. Our dream building was constructed and completed in the fall of 2003. We moved all our signage, equipment and tools in three days and opened our doors to clients with barely any disruption. The successful business at this location still operates today, under my ex-business partner's reign, almost right across the street from the bank that wouldn't talk to us about its potential.

I was happy to move to a smaller environment for the next phase of my career. Unfortunately, the salon owner had different plans and she expanded to a ten-chair salon with esthetic services, which is exactly what I had left. I was in a different place in my life and wanted a less-complicated environment. Though I stayed for several years, I did start to ponder the possibility of having a home salon and eventually, I made another dream of mine come true and opened the doors of my home studio in 2012. I love hairstyling in my home environment, and though I am nearing retirement age, I have no plans to retire anytime soon. I'm in my happy place.

The hairstyling industry is inherently a place that welcomes all into their workspaces. Statistics in both Canada and the United States report that ninety percent of salon personnel are women and ten percent are men, which strikes me as odd as I had never realized that we were so gendered lopsided. The first salon that I worked in was almost half men and half women. My salon team, however, was all women except for my male business partner. I have never had any issue with a male counterpart in the salon environment. Most of my distributorship sales consultants were men and are still to this day. I have no issues or complaints in this regard.

As a female, dealing with same-sex co-workers can sometimes be more difficult or intimidating than working with the opposite sex. As my hairstyling career moved to platform work with a manufacturer, the teaching bug was enhanced. I loved travelling and sharing knowledge with my fellow hairstylists. I wanted to teach! So, at the age of 46, I headed back to college to attain my Technical Vocational Teaching Certification, which is a requirement in my province to be able to teach in either a public vocational school program or a private school setting. It took me one and a half years to complete, all the while raising two young teens and working full time. With one course left to complete my studies, I was hired to teach a new program at a public school in a one-year term position. I made a few rookie errors, in the beginning, so at the suggestion of my director, I was mentored by one of my co-workers who taught in a different department. Together, we were unstoppable. My students loved what they were doing in the classroom setting and happily learned with success beyond my expectations. We sometimes grouped our learners for shared teaching regarding business or for them to learn from one another and exchange services. The school division that I was teaching in at the time had a phenomenal mentorship program. Three exceptional and experienced teachers working out of the divisional offices would visit groups of beginning teachers bi-weekly at their school locations and in their teaching environment. The purpose of these visits was to observe their teaching methods and coach them appropriately if required. I developed a remarkable relationship with my mentor. She marvelled at my work ethic and my teaching ability, which I had developed while teaching in the industry. Melding the two worlds together started me on a healthy teaching path in the school system. Or so I thought. Over the course of that year, my divisional mentor witnessed me being bullied, talked down to, and humiliated in front of my students by a co-worker. I was told that I was teaching "too much" to the learners. I was told that I wasn't giving enough homework. I was told to teach only what was in the textbook. I was told to leave unrealistic salon experiences or expectations out of it. One day, close to the end of the school year, I spent five hours with my graduating students, delivering a motivational session on how to build their business upon leaving the program. I had purposely chosen to do this in a classroom away from the salon setting, in a different part of the school. Once arriving back to a salon space at the end of the school day, the excited students were sharing information about what they had just learned, such as ideas about promoting themselves once they got to work behind their chairs. Sadly, my students were told by another co-worker that the information I had shared with them was inaccurate. They were told, "It will take you at least five years in the salon to make a healthy living, so don't give yourself false expectations about making a lot of money in your first few years." Anybody who has worked successfully in this business knows this not to be true. I was dumbfounded and horrified, as was my divisional mentor who had witnessed the delivery of this false information after having observed my presentation all day long. In my opinion, my role as a teacher was to lead by example, teach and share information both in the curriculum and industry-relevant. I wanted to share everything that I knew about the industry, particularly all my successes. I was leaving it up to them as to what information they wanted to retain. I wanted to give them everything that I had to help them succeed in the industry. It is a shame that, sometimes, women pit themselves against women in the workplace. Such behaviour does not help our cause for a positive work environment.

I believe that, in some cases, you must be thankful for the way that people treat you. It moves you in another direction, sometimes sooner than anticipated, usually on to better things. I have heard many times from an industry mentor, "Things don't happen to you; they happen for you." My permanent teaching position didn't pan out the way that I expected, however, it led me to work for a provincial organization that allowed me to develop programming for immigrants. These newcomers from the United States, many parts of Europe, China, the Philippines, and as far as Madagascar, came to our province with hairstyling training under their belt from their own countries. This created a need for all of them to be assessed and sometimes have to upgrade their knowledge of Canadian requirements to become hairstylists in our country. It was an honour mentoring these adventurous people. I would have been stellar at this job had I been able to speak languages from all around the world. I must admit, Google Translate came in mighty handy during these fourteen years.

I love delivering motivational speeches in school environments when invited into classrooms by friends or colleagues. Graduating students appreciate the information on business building and often laugh at my stories, both from behind my chair and in business. I find that sharing my experiences, in and out of the salon, brings great value to the beginning stylists heading into the industry. I love being in schools as a substitute teacher, delivering exactly what is required of me, and sometimes a little bit more. One of my favourite experiences to talk about is my involvement with the development of trade exams. I was asked to be part of a team that updates exams for the hairstyling trade in Ottawa. It is an extensive program that happens every four years. My involvement was to be part of a team that would ensure that the new exam questions were identical in both official languages. It is an intense three-day review, all part of an 18-month process for each trade, ending with four or five new versions of the Red Seal exam for certification in Red Seal trades. It was a long and tiring experience, yet wonderful to be included in the process. Opportunity is everywhere if you pay attention.

There are many options to create your own fun in this industry, such as when I participated in cutting hair for athletes at the 1999

Pan Am Games, which were held in Winnipeg. There is also ample opportunity to volunteer your time to cut hair for the homeless.

My dealings with distributorships, I must say, have been somewhat flawless over the years. Other than a few mishaps with product delivery, or a miscalculation on an invoice, I have nothing to complain about as far as respect for one another in our community of professionals goes.

As I write this book, we are in the year 2022. Are times changing in the world of business for women? Sexism in the workplace is, unfortunately, taking a long time to be rectified. Statistics still show that women are paid less than their male counterparts in many occupations, promoted less often and seldom at the top of a management team. My daughter has lived it at several workplaces, as have many of my clients. They talk to me about it, and while I would never disclose what any of them have had to endure, suffice it to say that women still have a long way to go before we can say that women in business are not treated any differently than men.

"The road to success is always under construction." *Lily Tomlin, actress, comedian, writer, and producer*

Inventions

Remember the guy that suggested I write a book so many years ago? Yup! Here he is again living on my pages. He and I have had many conversations over the last thirty-plus years, taking us all over the map on various topics. Our banter back and forth has brought about many discussions about non-existing products in the world, products that would have been, in our minds, handy to have at the time. Had those conversations taken place in today's world, I would bet that these ideas would have taken us to fantastic presentations in the studios of Dragon's Den or Shark Tank, two shows that were not on TV yet in the early 1990s.

We have collectively invented brilliant household items, personal items and children's toys. The reason that we are not rich and famous is that we never acted on any of them. Not one! We just talked about them… a lot… taking them from the brilliant idea stage to the point of proper design, functionality, the need for patents, colour variations and whether something would sell once it hit the market. We even got down to price points. We needed to

know what our investment was going to be to have these inventions developed and produced, and we needed to know if people
would be willing to pay for our much-needed gadgets. We never
discussed, however, how much money we'd potentially make if the
products did in fact hit the market, which, in retrospect, may have
been a great incentive to get some of these things into production.

Through our many deliberations, we put out such energetic
vibrations of success into the universe concerning these products
that they reached the minds of others, and many of our potential
inventions came to market within years of us "inventing them."
The funniest part about the eventual development of all these
spectacular products was watching my client's reaction when he
would come in for his regular hair appointment. I would deliver
the news to him that "something" was now new to the market
and wildly successful. This would lead to new discussions about
our lacklustre attitude toward acting on an idea, the need to start
investigating where to begin to develop our inventions, calcula-
tions of lost profits, and in the end, not getting recognition for
"our" inventions. We were brilliant and no one knew it! Coming
up with these product ideas, and feeling their need in the world,
was clearly on the minds of others who dared to bring them to
fruition. Good for them! How could you not cheer for the intel-
ligent and the successful? I believe in rippling goodness out into
the world, so I'd like to think that my client and I were part of these
inventions, wherever they came from, and that we were part of
the team of great people that put them on this earth for others to
enjoy, in the smallest of ways.

Allow me to share a little bit of our intelligence with you:

Our first invention, which was a huge one, came to me when I
was commenting on the fact that I was going to get someone in the
salon to apply some colour to my head following his appointment
and drive home to finish the process there myself so that I could
have some time with my kids and get a few things done around the

house. I am an open book and obviously share too much information with my clients sometimes. He remarked that he could see no gray hairs, and wondered why I wanted to do this, so I shared my little secret with him. Having inherited the genes of my father, who was very "salt and pepper" when he married my mother at the age of twenty-three, I saw the first gray hair on my head at the age of eighteen. At the age of twenty-three, I was diving into salt and pepper-ism myself. I was able to get away with temporarily covering my gray hair with semi-permanent hair colour. It was a great way to blend the gray with my natural hair colour while adding fun tones of red. After my son was born, I began using permanent hair colour to cover my rapidly graying hair. By this time, I was thirty years old.

Colouring gray hair is not a necessity in life, but as a hairstylist, I wanted to be a walking advertisement for hair colour, which I compared to a high-end, mature-age car salesperson driving the car they bought when they were eighteen. I didn't want to be like the vehicle, too new to be a valuable antique and too old to be seen on the lot of a high-end parking lot. Even today, I will admit that I am too vain to let my hair go natural.

My hair grows faster than average, so if I wanted to eliminate the visible re-growth, I could easily colour my hair every two to three weeks. Instead of going through the time and expense of doing this so often, I began buying dollar store eye shadows and brushes and started to apply the dark brown powder to my gray re-growth. I sometimes mixed two shades to get them to somewhat match the artificial colour that was currently on my head, and as a hairstylist, constantly changing. My partner-in-crime client commented on how brilliant this idea was, and that maybe, I had just invented something. Hot dang! It was truly a spectacular idea.

And the discussion deepened. What needed to be done to the dollar store eye shadow, to bring it to market in the hair world? What needed to be done to the shadow that was meant for eyes lids, to switch it up, and make it specific for applying to the regrowth of hair? How were we going to get it produced and into the hands of hair salons? Could we market it as a professional product, an in-between product offered to clients that wanted to extend their colour services? Would this be a good thing for the industry, or would it be a terrible one for stylists, now losing out on the frequency of hair colour services? My analysis was that, if I was doing this and I was still getting my colour services done on a regular schedule, why wouldn't other people? Who else would buy into this?

We wanted to help the people running out the door for work, those who had small children with not enough time on their hands, people who needed to go to an interview or an impromptu meeting, or anyone for that matter who didn't have the time for a complete hair service. We also didn't want to anger the hair world, offering something that was going to slow down business for stylists. I didn't want to be a hated target amongst my peers. "No one is going to buy this" was our most horrible conclusion.

As time passed, I saw companies spit these mineralized powders out, in mini eye shadow type pallets holding one or two shades, accompanied by a tiny brush, for application to gray hair, in all shades imaginable. The reason? To tie people over in between colour services. There have also been sprays, powders in little tubs with foam applicators, coloured conditioners, and hairline powder sponges developed over the years, and to this day, hold a very strong place in the market. Shelves of these products are in drugstores, grocery stores, and even on salon retail shelves. So, there was, and still is, a very clear market for such a product. A root touch-up product, invented by yours truly and my client, long before any of it ever hit the shelves of salons and retail stores everywhere. You're welcome!

Toys! Having five children between the two of us, all close to the same age, my client and I often talked about what activities they were involved in, what kind of sports they played, and what kind of toys they liked, their interests ever-changing as they age. I live in a part of the world where we are blessed with four seasons. Spring is sometimes a little messy when the snow melts, as the salt and sand spread to keep our streets and sidewalks safe over the winter becomes visible. Summer is typically hot, humid, and very enjoyable. Fall is my favourite season, whereby beautifully-dressed trees with many leaf colour variations line the streets as the weather becomes cooler. Winter brings the delivery of white fluffy snow and other elements such as cold and early darkness. This is the season that sometimes calls for strength as we adapt.

I had a winter appointment with my client at a time when our city was living through a horrid snow system attached to a terribly frigid cold snap, to the point where there was a weather warning on skin freezing in a matter of minutes should one venture outdoors. For those of you who live in the southern hemisphere, allow me to introduce you to Arctic temperatures in Canada. It has been documented as of late, that our city sometimes reaches sub-zero temperatures that are apparently colder than Mars. Yes, the planet Mars! Such temperatures make us very hardy human beings. This is the reason why most of us have closets full of long coats, shorter coats, thicker jackets, thinner jackets, and water-resistant jackets to wear on those days of sleet and snow. Fuzzy boots, water-resistant boots, insulated boots, fashion boots, baskets and drawers full of mittens, gloves, hats, and scarves of different thicknesses, made of various fabrics including my favourite, a synthetic, buttery soft yarn. If you like playing dress-up, this is the place to live in the winter months. On the days when you need to wrap your face up so that your skin doesn't freeze and succumb to frostbite, however, it's time to keep the kids inside the house to play, and by law, the younger ones need to be kept inside the building at recess time in schools. How do you occupy their time when a weather system prevents them from going outside for days? My client and I had ideas.

There is nothing like building a snowman outside. It is a rather easy, non-expensive and fun activity for any child living in these parts. Mother Nature often spits out the most perfect, wet and sticky snow to accommodate snowball fights, which can also become a fun pastime, if you can avoid a child from getting a black eye due to a badly thrown snowball or a sharpshooter with a strong arm. How about building a snow fort? Forts are a fantastic pastime and usually, last as a permanent playhouse until the temperatures rise and melt the structure. Snow sculptures are another fun thing to make if you are creative enough.

At one point in time, a severe snowstorm in November 1997 provided enough snow to turn our backyard into a winter slide sensation, starting on the deck attached to the house. We offered rides to all the neighbourhood kids where they had a blast except for a few rough finishes for some, slamming into the fence of our not-long-enough yard.

My client and I started to collaborate on a project that could bring all these activities into the house without causing a mess or harm. Indoor snowmen! Indoor snowballs! Indoor snow-fort bricks! I'll tell you right now that the reason we did not act on this great idea was because of storage space. We wanted this product to look like real snow products, with a possible Velcro type of attachment for easy assembly. Base, middle and head balls for the snowmen, easy block assembly for an individual design of forts, and of course, various sizes of balls for indoor snowball fights. Accessories for the snowmen/snowwomen could include "a corn-cob-pipe, and a button nose and two eyes made out of coal" like Frosty the Snowman.

Then we started to deliberate. Should we add hat variations and an optional carrot for the nose like Mr and Mrs. Potato Head? What sizes were needed to make it fun for the entire family? Should they come in a container the size of a Christmas tree, so that mom and dad could store this away with the Christmas decorations? Or should they be small enough to assemble on a table or the floor? Should the fabric be white like snow, or would this become a chore with the constant need to wash them? We decided that they needed to stay small enough for easy storage and compact playing space. This was not the purpose of the initial idea, as we wanted to simulate outdoor play, indoors. In the end, size ended up being an issue for us.

We took our idea and changed perspective, moving the concept to make snowmen kits out of felting, but then, in our eyes, the 3D "fun-ability" was gone, which took the wow factor out of it. The snowballs were on the table of development for a while, but as parents, we could envision a lamp or some other breakable trinket going down in the living room. We also did not want to encourage snowball fun turning into weapons against little brothers or sisters, and most certainly didn't want to be responsible for an irreplaceable antique being shattered! We struggled with the practicality of this invention. We knew that kids would have fun with them but didn't know what kind of space was required for the fun. Would it work in apartments or smaller homes? Was it something that grandma and grandpa would purchase for the little ones? Would parents appreciate that kind of purchase? Was it really an outdoor toy for when there was no snow or was it in fact, a great indoor toy?

With this idea, we started jumping to other seasons. Could we expand to assembly-required Easter bunnies, and Halloween pumpkin ensembles with abundant face options out of the same fabric? It was all getting confusing and confirmed the reason why we were not in the business of manufacturing toys.

It turns out that these were great ideas. A buildable snowman eventually came to market, made from felt-type material, with attachable eyes, noses, hats, scarves, and arms. The size of the 3D snowman was the size of a small child, which was the perfect size. A flat, non-3D version of a snowman made from felt also hit the toy market, as did a bag of artificial snowballs in many sizes. I have recently checked to see if they are still available on several websites. I can no longer find 3D snowmen, yet the bag of snowballs is still available for purchase, as are flat "build a snowman" felt kits.

Computers weren't readily available back then, so the idea of purchasing any kind of item online was not even in our vocabulary. Finding out that these products were available was through a sales consultant in the hair industry, toy flyers from larger companies and direct marketing sales catalogues that offered out-of-the-ordinary purchases. So, there you go, another great invention from my client and I went by the wayside!

Here is another one of our inventions that I would place in the category of "not our finest hour." This product was never going to hit the market, but worth the ink on these pages. The ridiculous discussion had us in stitches, laughing through tears at the thought of this being a permanent structure in both of our homes, if nowhere else. The idea came about when we were talking about a work team-building exercise, where you strategize together in small groups on how to duct-tape one of your co-workers to a wall. A real thing in the 1990s! There seemed to be something wrong with this picture; there is also a method to this madness. We digressed from there.

Again, with one, two, or all five of our children with "ants in their pants" behaviour, likely due to the winter weather again, we came up with another idea. We decided that a larger prototype for a playpen of some sort would be a great thing to keep older children, the two to four-year-olds, contained. It didn't take us long to figure out that this would not work in any size of the home, and it created a space where the children could hurt themselves in the confined space. Putting them in an empty room would have brought the same result, rendering our invention unessential, also bringing to the forefront that this may be illegal behaviour on our part.

So, how could we come up with something that wasn't going to have us arrested and still be fun for our children? This took us to the idea of an inflatable bouncy-castle type of wall structure, which would need to be weighted at the bottom for safety, and could lean up against a wall, with the other side of the exposed wall made of Velcro. The structure would come with adjustable Velcro suits for the kids to wear so that the kids could throw themselves onto the wall and stick. We thought that the kids would have fun running and jumping up into the wall, with their weight being absorbed by the thickness of the wall. Of course, the wall would also need to come with a mat system to catch the kids that didn't stick. Maybe even letting the wall structure lay on the floor could have been a fun activity, with the kids getting great exercise in rolling around with the resistance of the Velcro suits on the Velcro wall. A question arose. If they stick to the wall in the upright position, how would they get down?

The idea of this being a large toy then switched to becoming a parenting tool, to keep the children in one spot for a limited time. How long would it take before they began asking to come down? If nothing else, this absurd idea and silly talk about a Velcro wall during this hair appointment offered great laughter therapy for both of us, and a few nearby stylists and clients who got in on the conversation about this invention determined that this invention was never going to be. I often think that I missed my calling on many fronts. I can say, however, that the development and manufacturing of toys were never one of the options on my horizon.

Fun fact: This talent for inventions comes naturally to me. My mother's father was a sheet metal worker. At some point in his life, he invented a drum that rotated, had dry oatmeal inside and was used for cleaning furs or fur coats. I don't have the back story on this invention, but I feel that it seems plausible for the 1930s.

He started his own business, which was eventually taken over by his sons, my uncles, and then their sons, my cousins. As is the story about the drum with the oatmeal, the following story is also documented in a genealogy book that was researched and written by one of my uncles, with a little help from my aunt, his younger sister. My grandfather worked for a company named MacDonald Bros, and in 1930, he was sent to do work for them in Prince Albert, Saskatchewan. My grandmother followed behind shortly afterwards, by train, with nine children. During his time in Prince Albert, my grandfather invented the humidifier and the company he worked for began manufacturing it. The background to this discovery is that, as woodstoves and indoor fireplaces were in homes for heating and cooking, it was recognized that a cauldron of water sitting on the stove would add humidity into the home on cold winter days, promoting healthy air in the home. The owner of the shop, along with my grandfather, made their way from Prince Albert to Winnipeg, to seek backers for the invention and to have the humidifier patented. While they were there, my grandfather received some bad advice from who knows who to hold out for more money. While doing so, someone copied the design and had it patented. At one point, he told my grandmother that he had lost everything. He eventually left this company to start Northern Roofing, with his oldest son joining in on the adventure. To those of you who have humidifiers in your homes, whether it is to add comfort from electric heat, or to breathe better when you have a cold, you're welcome!

"The way to get started is to quit talking and begin doing." *Walt Disney*

Let Your Hair Down

O ne of my long-time desires was fulfilled in 2014 with the purchase of an antique barber chair – an authentic 1920 Koken chair constructed of iron, steel, and porcelain. Manufactured in the early 1900s in St. Louis, Missouri, these chairs have working hydraulics and reclining backs. They were designed for comfort, integrity and classic style. Ernest Koken is the man behind the modern-day barber, stylist and dental chair.[1]

This chair came with a charming story. I purchased it from the grandson of a barber. The chair was stored in his mother's garage for years after her father's passing. Twenty years after his grandfather's passing, the grandson asked his mother for the chair. He spent a good amount of money to have the metal pieces of the chair re-chromed, oodles of time refurbishing it by stripping off the white painted oak to a detailed wood finish, and hours reupholstering the cushions and headrest. In his efforts, he misplaced one part of the chair. I bought the chair knowing this, with the

---

1   thebarberden.net

intention of locating a calf rest, or alternately, building something to fit the empty spot. Though this brings forth other challenges, such as finding and matching the exact fabric that has been put on the chair cushions, I love this project and look forward to completing it. What became my favourite thing about this purchase are two signs that the son offered to me, in exchange for their safe-keeping. I am now the caretaker of a hand-painted wood sign with the name of his grandfather's shop - Princess Beauty Parlor - with the words "Walk-In" painted on the bottom right-hand corner. The second sign is printed on an over-sized, thick cardboard stock dated August 10, 1953, and lists the following services and prices:

Haircuts, Adults		.75
Brush cuts, Adults	Extra	.15
Haircuts, Children under 14		.50
Ladies' Neck Clip		.35
Shave		.50
Hair Tonic		.25
Vibrator on Scalp		.25
Shampoo		.75 & up
Facial Massage		.75 & up
Hair Singe		.75
Razors Honed		.75

I love the fact that shampoo was as valuable, if not more, than a haircut, something that I still believe today. I love the fact that the small print at the bottom of this sign states that on Saturdays, the price of children's haircuts would be the same as adults. Saturdays were then, as they are now, the busiest day of the week for most hairstylists and most notably this barber, and he wanted to bring in as many 75 cent sales as he could to this eclectic chair.

This chair symbolizes so much for me and is why it was so important that I buy it. It was a gift FROM me TO me. I searched for many years to find one that I liked and had a stash of cash put away for when the time came. I have since unintentionally added to this "barber" collection by receiving the gift of a box of accessories from one of my dear friends. He had been storing three of his father's razors, a hone and a strop, (both instruments to sharpen vintage razors) a soap cup for shaving, and shaving soap in a porcelain container, never used, still hanging on to the slight fragrance of years gone by. I cried happy tears when I received these nostalgic gems. I then added two more tools to the mix: one antique, manual neck-trimmer gifted to me by my mother-in-law when I graduated from hairstyling, and a pink comb with a built-in razor blade that my mother used on my dad's head, right after she washed his hair and treated it with a liquid bluing agent. The blade on that comb from the 60s was rusted beyond the pale, so it was safely disposed of but the comb is still intact. I am hoping that this collection will be for the eyes of many once I accomplish my vision and get it all into a display cabinet beside my prized chair in the basement. This project is something that keeps me busy aside from my work and home life. Doing something you love to do and that speaks to your heart is a good way to let your hair down, something that is necessary for all our lives.

My profession allows anyone who walks through a salon door for service to sit in a stylist's chair and let their hair down, literally and metaphorically. It's a safe place to sit in silence if one wants to decompress or a place to speak about anything that is on their mind. I have heard stories. I have been asked opinions. I have been asked for suggestions or advice for various situations. Often, when clients move away, they ask for recommendations or a hairstylist's name in their new location. Someone moving to Minneapolis once asked for a referral, and upon receiving the names of two stylists that I knew who worked in her vicinity, she responded with, "Perfect, now all I need is to find a doctor and a dentist!" It made me smile to know that a hairstylist was higher on her priority list than the medical professionals.

Letting your hair down! I have experienced it on many occasions. I have watched both happy and sad tears flow. I have nursed headaches with peppermint oil and temple massages. I have heard about new romances and tenderly celebrated the end of toxic relationships. I have been given details of many stunning weddings and social occasions, and, unfortunately, some horrible social gatherings, from the good food to the bad food, the sometimes badly behaved and not so classy at a time when class was required of them. I have navigated awkward conversations and stayed silent if I did not agree with political views, religious beliefs, and other newsworthy affairs, all on the docket of subjects to avoid when working as a professional hairstylist. I have walked through all stages of life with many clients. I am the captive audience of those who sit and divulge freely about everyone and anyone in their lives, everything and anything. It is my honour to listen attentively. I am sure, however, that any hairstylist will admit to falling into a mild trance in the middle of a story on occasion. There is a time of day when this just happens.

I often wonder who is benefitting from the appointment more, my clients or me. Most of the time, I love to hear all about whatever my clients deem important to tell me. Depending on the subject matter, it does become overwhelming at times. I truly believe that my client's appointment is all about them, therefore their time, and as such, they can talk about (or not talk about) whatever they want. As for me, that is what downtime is for.

One of my sisters used to own a cottage where the family was always welcomed and invited. On the weekends when we would be heading out with the kids to spend time with nature, family and friends, and great food, I would work the Saturday morning in the salon, and then come home to change, gather my things and we would leave right after lunch for the two-hour drive. My kids were always so excited to get there that they would hop in the car as soon as I arrived home from the salon. I would barely get in the house and they were already buckled into their seats and then complain that they had to wait for me before we hit the road. It was funny and annoying time after time. Once we arrived, my husband would help unload food, bags and pillows from the car, and promptly head outside with the kids for a bunch of adventures. The first task on my son's list was to find a walking stick that doubled as a fire-poking stick. My daughter always kept an eye out for deer to feed and threw wildflower seeds in the tall grass for them. They would walk to the beach to check out the water and were always on the hunt for evidence of bears on the path, which was very intriguing for the five and seven-year-olds. I have so many pictures of them doing all these things and barely any of myself because I was always the one holding the camera. I'm ok with that, as these precious memories are engrained in my mind forever. While all of this was happening, I would be inside unpacking food and settling us into our designated bedroom. My kids learned quickly that it was happy hour somewhere in the world, which always meant that it was time for a snack and some juice for them. Friendly neighbours gathered around a fire outside for interesting and fun conversations. I, having finished a week of work just minutes before leaving for the lake, would almost always grab a book and sit inside the cottage to decompress from the happy noise of the salon. I did this for hours on end, avoiding all others in and outside the cabin. In fact, I was once carried out of the sunroom, the chair that I was sitting in included, and transplanted around the fire so that I could be part of the conversation! This will always remain for me a funny and cherished memory. Upon landing in my new location, I explained to my sister's friend, who had brainstormed the idea to move me outside, that I have a job that requires me to do constant talking and even more attentive listening. He empathized with the demands of the job and the energy required, and then proceeded to say, "But you're like the cottage snob (he may have used another word) that doesn't talk to anyone when you get here." I burst out laughing, as did everyone else, and I suddenly understood what he was saying. I was at the cottage, exactly where I was meant to be at that moment, and I needed to be present. It was time to be with friends and family, not alone with a book, albeit, to me, both are perfect scenarios. The point of the matter is that I needed to let my hair down.

I, along with my co-workers, have let our hair down many times for moments of detox, moments of pure silliness, and sometimes embarrassing pleasures, both within and away from our work environment. From a work perspective, it is a definite necessity.

My first salon had a staff of nine, comprised of eight stylists and one receptionist. When we moved to the larger location, we expanded to a staff of sixteen, which included ten stylists, two estheticians, a massage therapist, a receptionist and various rock star assistants. It wasn't uncommon for us to break out in song when something good came on the radio. A few of us could harmonize, causing some of us to stop working, with stylists and clients alike appreciating the free concert. There were no streaming options back then and nobody had time to change cassette tapes or CDs, so radio music it was. The moments in between clients gave us the opportunity to up our game by singing into one's hairbrush before cleaning it from debris, or the tip end of a curling or flat iron as it was being unplugged from the wall. The hot tools were magnificent as they mimicked a corded microphone. By far, my favourite singing prop was always the broom handle. The imaginary microphone on a stand allowed me to transform into my inner singing star in nanoseconds while gathering hair off the floor. Whoever was on the radio, I became them. And if I had lacklustre singing skills, I made up for it by flipping my hair back and forth and side to side. I did whatever it took to create a great performance.

The staff room in the new salon was substantially larger than the old salon. The old one was a five-by-five-foot square cubby with no door, and not remembering the exact measurements, I may be exaggerating its size. Tiny. It had a three-cubic-foot fridge and two chairs. That's it. When more than two people were trying to put some food into their stomachs in between clients, it was a tight squeeze, and I was thankful for getting along with my peers, and our clients, who were sometimes transposed there while their colours were processing. When we moved, we expanded to an eight-by-sixteen-foot rectangle. Again, not quite sure of the exact measurements. It was where we now mixed colours for our clients, and we had an actual table and four chairs to sit and eat in between appointments. This larger area even had space set aside for kitchen supplies, our coats and bags, and a cupboard dedicated to colour and other salon supplies. It allowed for more opportunities to be together and have room to spare. It wasn't unusual to have a tiny dance party while in there, with or without other colleagues, singing or no singing included. The dead space in front of the cabinets allowed just enough room for body movement. We now had a place to perform stellar dance moves, yoga stretches, dramatized film and theatre re-enactments, model poses, and of course, just plain silliness. It was our sacred space that allowed for plenty of belly laughs, which truly is the best medicine. The public washroom door was across from the opening to the staff room, so periodically, we would get caught by clients in our crazed moments. And still, they kept coming back, even after witnessing the nonsense, accepting that our personalities created the behaviour.

Aside from singing and dancing in the salon to entertain ourselves, there always seemed to be some form of unorthodox basketball game happening when it came time to throw towels in the laundry basket or the washing machine. No talent required! Just childlike behaviour that made the day brighter for no other reason than being happy and loving our work, cleaning tasks included. One notable incident that happened in that dreaded laundry room was a creature nibbling its way through the exhaust vent of the dryer from the outside and finding a nice place to sleep overnight in a load of towels that were left behind. Our poor assistant came into the salon the next morning, turned on the dryer to fluff up the cooled down towels, and when she reached inside to retrieve the now warm towels, she grabbed on to a squirmy little mouse! She screamed and ran! I was happy not to be in the vicinity and was no help at all. The mouse was retrieved by another staff member who was nearby and set the little guy free. The towels then went straight into the garbage for fear of hantavirus disease. This may have been an extreme precaution, but I didn't know how long that little creature had been living in the fluff, so out they went. I also proceeded to clean the dryer thoroughly with a disinfectant.

Hair shows are the tradeshow experience for hairstylists, with pizzazz! They often become a very scary thing for clients as in the days following these shows, we are all eager to experiment with the newly-learned cuts, colour placement and techniques, and of course, our clients are always the best models. Before I became a hairstylist, I tagged along to many hair shows with my girlfriends just to get a feel for the industry. Hair shows bring manufactur-ers together to present seasonal trends to like-minded people and include brilliant platform artists who have honed their artistry, showing us their innovative nature on a stage backed by lights, music and flair. They inspire and get the hairstyling community's creative juices flowing. Hair shows offer opportunities to mingle, get educated and shop for new, though not always necessarily needed, tools and equipment. They also create fine opportunities to share lunches, dinners and a few cocktails with old and new friends. Most hair shows run on Sundays and Mondays, which used to be the typical days off in the industry and are known as our weekends. After working a five-day workweek in the salon, adding the two days in between two weeks for a hair show extends your work life to a twelve-day stretch. It is worth making this work, however, and not hard to manage once or twice a year, and most importantly, it's a great way for hairstylists to let their hair down.

There have been times when the salon seemed to be deserted with most of the staff congregating on a plane heading to Montreal, Toronto, or other large cities. Here, the trade shows were much larger and offered broader education and top-name manufacturers. The larger the cities, the bigger the venues. I had the pleasure of sharing a trip to Tampa Bay, Florida with one of my team members for a five-day seminar led by one of the industry's finest. It was intense learning and refreshing at the same time. We had a few fun moments on the way there, like accidentally using dark brown eyeliner to line my lips instead of my pink lip pencil. A table of travellers in the airport was looking at me and scratching their heads, trying to figure out what kind of statement I wanted to make! Once in Tampa Bay, we settled into a fascinating tower hotel by the ocean, a treat for Canadian prairie girls in February, and met wonderful people from all over the USA and Canada, some of whom I still communicate with today. The full days of learning were exceptional, always interesting and of great value. Having separated from my roommate one evening after dinner, I made my way back to our room to find her cleaning up the mess caused by a shattered bottle of nail polish on the tile floor in the bathroom. I was overtaken by the fumes of the nail polish remover and didn't quite know how she was still conscious. She had apparently been on her hands and knees for some time already, failing to remove all of it from the grout. Being slightly intoxicated from the fumes may have caused her to order a large pot of coffee and a giant-sized piece of chocolate cake at ten o'clock at night! I mean really, who has coffee and chocolate cake just before bed? I laughed when the hotel employee wheeled in a fancy cart with her room service order just as I was settling into bed.

A hair show once took the entire salon team on a road trip to Fargo, North Dakota. I decided to be one of the drivers and was thrilled to be travelling with two of my stylists for the three-hour ride. Upon arrival, we needed to get American money into our wallets to have small bills for incidentals. We decided to check out a new, at the time, drive-through Automated Teller Machine. ATMs were old news, but the drive-through versions were the novel idea of not having to get out of the car, which seemed to be genius. We located one in a large retail mall parking lot which included a brick-and-mortar bank, so I made my way around it and ended up driving toward the ATM in the wrong direction. I came face-to-face with a carload of people coming out of the drive-through lane who must have thought that this Canadian girl had completely lost her mind. The clarity of people's facial expressions is evident when you drive the hood of your vehicle nose-to-nose with theirs! I'm not sure why I reached in my purse at that exact moment for my lip balm as I backed up to let them through. I guess I was letting the nonsensical moment sink in. The uncontrollable laughter in my vehicle from that point on was the start of an incredible weekend with downtime, getting to know your fellow hairstylists while out of town time, "YMCA" dance time and a whole lot of bonding with the best group of hairstylists anyone could ask to work with.

Mannequin heads… these handy tools can create a lot of opportunities to let our hair down. We name them, we talk to them, we have them talk to each other, we grab them by the neck and shake them upside down, and that is just for starters. One of my best memories is of an all-day cutting class held on a Sunday. Most of us took our own vehicles to the class as we all had to be at many different locations for family dinners afterwards. As we convoyed home from the class, we hit a red light at a busy intersection, with four lanes of traffic travelling each north, south, east, and west. One of the stylists, who was rocking out to some loud dance music, picked up her newly coiffed mannequin head by the neck, stretched out her arm holding the doll head, and positioned it as though the mannequin was sitting in the passenger seat. She began moving her to the beat of the music with her hair flailing all over the front of the vehicle. From far away, you would have thought that someone in the car was having the time of her life! As we gathered at the same intersection, we all did the same. The ten mannequin heads dancing in the seats of our cars produced much laughter on our part and caused surrounding cars to ponder what in the world was going on! This is one of my favourite let your hair down moments that I will not soon forget.

Taking part in industry competitions is a creative way of working your magic with added pizazz. There are skills competitions where students can demonstrate learned accuracy and precision on male and female mannequin heads which I have had the opportunity and pleasure to judge locally for the past ten years. There used to be plenty of live competitions which typically took place at hair shows, where pre-coloured human models were taken to a recommended style conducive to the competition. Sadly, our region hasn't had those types of hair shows or competitions for many years. Photography competitions require a lot of planning and preparation and end with a photo shoot with an accredited photographer and three or more willing models. I participated in industry competitions ten years in a row, making it to the semi-finals eight times and the finals once. Our salon was recognized nationally one year for the Community Service Award. Road trips to these award dinners year after year were spectacular experiences. These black-tie events are the "Academy Awards" of the hair industry.

Our salon put on an annual, one-day barbecue in our parking lot and adjacent yard, with proceeds benefitting The Children's Wish Foundation. Once we tired of the barbecue model, we moved to evening fashion shows at a local piano bar, with our clients modelling clothes from local clothing companies. Of course, each model had stylish hair creations by our team. Over the course of eight years, these annual events raised over $25,000 for the charity. Supported by local celebrities and radio personalities, these events and the organization required were quite fulfilling and in the category of feeling as good as when you let your hair down.

As a group, we also took part in fantasy competitions that were hosted by one of our local suppliers. Up to a maximum of twenty salons were able to compete whereby creative geniuses built monumental hair pieces on their models. Temples, animal figurines, flowers and unicorns all made from hair graced the stage. We participated with "Lady Luck" one year and we placed second. Our receptionist was our model, and we had her parading down the stage in a white and purple sequinned bathing suit, a purple boa, and high heels. Her headdress was a white and purple extravaganza, featuring heart, spade, diamond, and club shapes placed amongst purple and white tubular shapes on a large glittery Styrofoam platform, all covered with hair, accompanying large white feathers. The following year, we presented with an "Aphrodite" theme. As plain as the headdress seemed, it was so heavy because of the glue holding the hair in place that it was hard for the model to balance properly. "Go big or go home" isn't always the winner in these types of competitions if the model must hang on to what is placed on her head. The most applause we ever received in this competition was when one of our hairstylists, already sporting a short haircut, agreed to let us colour her hair in seven vibrant colours to mimic a beach ball. She was dressed in a bodysuit, and her headdress was an octopus with removable arms. As she paraded down the runway to music, she ripped off one octopus tentacle at a time when the appropriate beat in the music occurred. When the eighth one came off, she ripped off the body of the octopus worn as a hat, revealing her colourful head of hair and began a gymnastic routine, ending with a few backflips on the runway. It was amazing! No prizes were awarded to us that night. Nevertheless, we appreciated the loud support from the crowd.

Co-workers play a large part in the happiness of a workplace no matter the industry. I don't know a lot of hairstylists that stay in this line of work if they are miserable. If you are that discontented, you typically decide to leave or direct your energy into a different branch of the industry. In my world, it is important to be able to laugh with coworkers, confide in them and trust each other. There is something to be said for sitting in a colleague's chair and trusting their judgement as to what to do with your hair when it's time for a change. Becoming your co-worker's guest is an indescribable bonding experience. You soon learn how they see you. Almost every weekend in the salon, at least one of our stylists would sit in each other's chair for a "do" for a night out, an unwritten perk of being a hairstylist. Often, we would even apply colour to each other's hair in between clients, sometimes needing to rinse it off ourselves. We happily became each other's stylists, teachers, assistants and mentors.

I have been blessed with the best team members over my career, where letting my hair down with them was an honour and a blessing. As I wind down my career by working in my home salon alone, I often miss the comradery of days gone by. To this point, when the opportunity presents itself for us to get together, whatever the occasion, we have managed to do so, yet not often enough. In the spring of 2017, we gathered at a colleague's home for a splendid lunch full of emotional conversations. One from our group, recently diagnosed with cancer was our reason to gather to support each other that day, and mostly to support her. Within a few months, our beautiful "Red" ended up in the hospital, ultimately being transferred to palliative care where some of us had the honour of caring for her. It was horrible to watch this delicate forty-seven-year-old soul depart the land of the living. She is now our reason to gather on a patio every July to remember the good times that we shared with her over the years.

Let your hair down. A necessity in life. What do you do to let your hair down?

"Girl, put your records on, tell me your favorite song
You go ahead, let your hair down
Sapphire and faded jeans
I hope you get your dreams
Just go ahead, let your hair down
You're gonna find yourself somewhere, somehow"
Lyrics to "Put Your Records On" by Corinne Bailey Rae

Hairstyling in the Midst of a Pandemic

There was never a plan to include a chapter concerning the pandemic in this book. Writing page after page about COVID19 and the effects this insidious virus has had on every aspect of society did not appeal to me in the least. The last two years have been unprecedented and will go down in history as one of those extraordinary times, and so it stands to reason that I describe how it affected the hair industry.

In one way or another, we have all been touched by this pandemic, and from a personal and career standpoint, it has affected hair salons and stylists around the world. Members of our industry, like so many others, have had to re-think how we work, enhance how we clean, and be mindful of government-guided restrictions, regulations and protocols.

Frankly, I'm not quite sure when any of my clients are ever going to see my face again. I surprisingly don't mind wearing a mask while working. Being as near to my clients as I am while cutting or colouring their hair or giving them a shampoo, I feel a higher level of safety with my mask and shield. I have clients in the medical field who have commented on the fact that I am closer to my clients' faces than they are in proximity to their patients. The mask is doing its job by keeping germs at bay and let's be real, it is containing all kinds of odours that may emanate from one's mouth. Masks can sometimes feel hot on the face, especially when you are menopausal, and having them on your face for a long period takes some getting used to. Then again, they hide the fact that I mumble to myself more than I was aware, they prevent me from showing a sometimes-grumpy looking face, and they keep me from spitting things out of my mouth as I've been known to do.

In the latter part of the year 2019, rumblings of an unknown virus on the other side of the planet were beginning to get my attention, partially because I had a girlfriend planning to leave for Vietnam in January with her family for a three-week vacation. Reports were circulating from the Municipal Health Commission of China about clusters of pneumonia in Wuhan, Hubei province. At her December hair appointment, I shared my concern about her leaving, which was all that I could do. There is no way of stopping anyone's dream vacation. As information about the "Wuhan flu" continued to emerge, the Government of Canada implemented signage about this health security risk in three major airports on January 17th, 2020: Vancouver, Toronto, and Montreal, cities that provided direct flights to China. My girlfriend and her family were on their way to Vietnam on the 26th of January. With the twelve-hour time difference from here in Winnipeg to where she was in Vietnam, we communicated in the evening for me, when it was morning for her, or vice versa. We had several face-to-face chats, and not once did she ever mention that she was not well. She wasn't.

On February 2nd, 2020, the Canadian Armed Forces planned to bring back Canadian citizens out of Wuhan, once given authorization by China. On February 21st, a chartered flight of 131 Canadians who were quarantined on a cruise ship in Japan after an outbreak was brought to an army base in Trenton, Ontario, Canada for additional screening. From there, they were transported to Cornwall, Ontario for further quarantine. People with this "flu" had officially landed in our country at a time when there were still many unknowns about its capabilities.

On March 11th, 2020, the World Health Organization declared the virus, now called COVID19, was officially causing a worldwide pandemic. I heard this announcement on the radio as I drove home from an out-of-town substitute teaching job, a forty-eight-minute ride from the school to my house, which gave me ample time to think. It gave me an open highway to strategically organize my thoughts about what was currently going on, not only around the world but in my own life at that moment in time. You see, my daughter was pregnant with her second child, with a due date of March 20th. Plans were for my husband and I to take care of our almost-three-year-old granddaughter and the family dog while mom and dad went into the hospital for the delivery of the new baby. As the week went on and as news about the pandemic emerged, I was feeling quite panicked. Not only was I periodically exposed to students in schools, but I also had a stream of clients coming into my home salon. I was also mildly distraught at the fact that my husband, who was a high school principal, was working with approximately sixty staff members and surrounded by 640 students daily, all going home at the end of the day to their environments and in contact with their friends and families. This is a small size in comparison to other high schools in the city, but when I thought of all these contacts we had regularly, I couldn't help but think that this would not be good when I was about to be around a child, a brand-new baby, a mom who just delivered the baby and a dad. And let's not forget the dog. No one knew at this point if or how this virus affected animals.

On one of my daughter's last visits to her doctor before having her baby, she was told that they didn't know if her husband was going to be allowed to attend the birth. She called me in a panic and told me that if her husband was not going to be allowed in the hospital with her, she was going to have a home birth. I understood what she was saying and why. Not many women want to be alone while in labour. They want their partners nearby for love and support. Even though I'd had two children of my own, and I was her mom, I did not feel equipped to help with the birth, though I was honoured that she thought of me to help. I, like so many others, suddenly felt that the world was caving in on us.

As the unknowns of the virus continued to make the news, my panic mode, which was already heightened, started to reach new levels. That being said, my anxiety was beginning to enhance my creativity, all to keep everyone safe. I told my husband that should my daughter approve, I was going to pack my bags and move into their basement until this chaos was over. This way, I could take care of their entire household while they went to the hospital. I could cook and clean, which is a great stress reliever for me, and come home when the pandemic would be over, or whenever they no longer needed me, whichever came first. I had ordered myself a new KitchenAid stand mixer, which could easily be moved to their kitchen to make fresh buns and other daily bakery-type treats. The first thing out of my husband's mouth was, "When am I going to see you again?" I was stunned. We deliberated as to what that scenario would look like. I knew that I wanted to help my daughter after the birth, the same way that I did with her firstborn. I also didn't want to be going from our house to theirs with the potential of carrying the virus either from my husband's work environment or my clients. I was in a dilemma.

My daughter, who was already on leave from work, came for a visit that Friday. I mentioned that we had been talking about me potentially moving into their basement leading up to the birth, with a large suitcase of clothes to accommodate for as long as they needed me. My husband would be on standby to purchase whatever we required, if anything, or deliver more clothing, as we only live six minutes away from each other. She informed me that she and my son-in-law had already talked about the possibility, and at this point, they were still taking it one day at a time. That Sunday morning, with the baby's due date less than a week away, I felt powerless. This virus was picking up speed in headline news with the death tolls rising around the world by the minute. All I could think of was that the smooth and well-thought-out plans for this new baby's arrival were crumbling at every turn. Watching me burst into tears at the thought of what was headed our way, my husband placed a phone call to his assistant superintendent to explain our family situation, which at that point we had labelled as a crisis. He asked permission to work from home, with the support of his vice-principal, who would still be physically in the school with the other staff and students. He would be in constant communication from his home base. The request was approved on March 15th. The next day, March 16th, border restrictions between Canada and the United States were announced. Non-essential travel was not allowed and fourteen-day self-isolation was required upon entry for those returning home from vacations or work-related trips. With that information, I decided to cancel my appointments for the upcoming week. I just did it and the thought of doing this didn't even phase me. This was the first effort in keeping our house free of any outside germs. I contacted my clients to inform them that I was closing my salon until further notice and continued calling, soon cancelling four weeks of upcoming appointments. On March 20th, my future grandchild's due date, Manitoba declared a state of emergency, shutting down all non-essential businesses, which included hair salons. And just like that, I had no income.

That Saturday, while we waited for the arrival of our little peanut, my husband began painting my salon to keep himself busy, and I began cleaning everything in sight. Two of my girlfriends living in British Columbia, also hairstylists, and both married to men in sales, were now at home, unable to work, with no income or restitution to pay their home bills or their salon rent. We decided to connect with them through FaceTime that Saturday evening. This was the first of many calls with friends and family, near and far, keeping the lines of communication open so that we could focus on something other than the pandemic, and check on each other's wellbeing, now that the world was sitting still.

My daughter was visiting almost every day to get herself out of the house. This gave her daughter a new place to play, as daycares and schools were now also closed. Students were in full swing of remote learning and parents were left to manage their little ones at home, with daycares operating strictly for essential working staff. On March 24th, our province enacted the Emergency Response Act and enforced several measures, including social distancing, mask-wearing and consistent hand washing. It all seemed too much to absorb. These three measures very quickly became repeated steps to take, and eventually, the norm for almost everyone.

The next day, on Wednesday, March 25th, after a short morning visit, my daughter returned home and not long after, her water broke. The time had come! She called her husband first, who had thankfully been given the OK to attend the delivery at the hospital, and then she called me so that I could pick up my granddaughter and the dog. My son-in-law arrived at their house minutes after I did, and very quickly thereafter, they were off to the hospital. I stayed at the house for a few hours to do dishes, clean up washrooms, tidy up toys, wipe down door handles, wash floors and pack up all that we needed for the next few days, and then made my way home with my precious cargo. The original plan to bring our granddaughter to the hospital to meet her new sibling was cancelled, but we were happy for her to meet her baby brother through an early morning FaceTime the next day. That Friday morning, they were discharged from the hospital. We let them settle in before bringing their daughter and dog home to them. I entered the house, where the new protocol of washing our hands upon entry became standard. I was also, for the first time, entering their home with a mask covering my nose and mouth. The hospital had advised not to let anyone hold the baby, or get closer than six feet, so for the first three weeks of our new grandson's life, we watched him with tear-filled eyes from chairs positioned at a proper distance from the couch, where the new little family sat. Many of their friends and extended family were coming over for "window" visits, which was such a special and sad thing to watch, adorning gifts, baking, or meals, left on the doorstep for us to pick up once they left. I was taking pictures to document this unbelievable phenomenon so that they had a record of who came by.

Nine days after the lockdown, and two days after our grandson was brought home, I celebrated my 60th birthday on a family ZOOM call with my four sisters, brothers-in-law, nieces, nephews, and their children. There are forty-five of us including the little people. My daughter and her family were on the call, introducing their new and tiny human to the rest of the family. It was a cherished moment for all of us, though there was a mishap in the new family's home. A beverage landed on the floor, and both new parents spent most of the time cleaning up while the rest of us all talked in unison, no one knowing how this ZOOM thing was working.

With my salon closed, and my clients not coming to join me for coffee and chats, my grandkids and my daughter became my purpose. I made my way to them every morning. I became the one in charge of household chores, making lunch, sometimes preparing dinner, and then heading back home at the end of the day, where my husband had been working in his pop-up office in the basement all day long. His days were getting longer as the world of teaching flipped on a dime to accommodate students around the world.

On April 6th, 2020, an announcement came from the Canadian government, introducing the Canada Emergency Response Benefit, which soon came to be known as CERB. For the first time in my hard-working life, I would be collecting a government employment insurance benefit.

Hairstylists in Canada are guided by federal and provincial governing bodies specifically known as the Interprovincial Standards Red Seal Program, and each province has apprenticeship branches that set common standards for tradespeople. While hairstylists no longer have an association in Manitoba, which I had the privilege of experiencing when I first started hairstyling years ago, we do have a great group of people that started a private page through Facebook, offering a place of support for like minds to banter back and forth on many topics. This group was very active during this time, with stylists talking about take-home product sales, take-home colour kits, and how CERB and other government support programs were going to help us through this time. There was a sense of comradery among us. It was also a great place to go for advice and information on grants and various support programs as they became available to us.

By the middle of April, I was settling into my new routine of manning my household, with my husband continuing to work at home, most days starting at 7:00 am, and sometimes climbing up the stairs ten, eleven or even twelve hours later. The habit of going to my daughter's house to help with the little ones was my new normal away from the salon. My days started with a shower at home, continuing with extravagant hand washing at my daughter's. Grocery shopping became an event, disinfecting almost everything brought into the house. My husband became our designated shopper. He would strip down at the door after picking up grocery items and throw his clothes directly into the washing machine where they were immediately washed. He would then jump in the shower. My son-in-law was practicing the same protocol once he returned home from work, going directly downstairs to shower before hugging his wife and children, all to keep his family safe. I was happy that my son was also able to work remotely from his home during this time. I was keeping in contact with many of my clients, all of whom seemed to be living the same life as us, as far as cleaning and disinfecting were concerned. Some were ordering groceries online, while others were having their children shop for them.

My grandson was three weeks old before we could hold him while adorning a mask and wearing a makeshift gown made from my son-in-law's long-sleeved shirts. Thank goodness he is 6'4", which made this an easy process to get the gown on and off.

By this time, clients began calling me for colour consultations, asking if they could pick up a colour for their hair so that they could give themselves colour treatments at home, which many salons were offering to their clients. Take-home colour kits! Salons were creating liability waiver forms to protect themselves with the distribution of these personalized kits. It was a great way to create income while we were in limbo, waiting for governmental financial support to kick in. Personally, I did not feel comfortable handing over professional colour to my clients and made the decision not to offer that as an option, with a few exceptions. I have two clients who are regular winter month travellers and I have been supplying colour to them for years. Once they reach their destinations, professional stylists applied their colours for them. They were the first to call and ask if I would give them colour during the lockdown. I decided to make an exception for these two clients. Phone calls continued to come from others, some just to say hello, but most asking for help with their hair colour status. Eventually, I gave in to three more long-time clients and provided them with the option to pick up hair colour from me if they promised to explicitly follow my detailed instructions. These three pick-ups included a phone call to clarify instructions, a FaceTime call to supervise the application process to prevent a domestic dispute between husband and wife, and a second FaceTime call with a girlfriend and her plus-one, who was applying her colour and cutting her hair! This new way of helping my clients was sometimes very serious business, sometimes funny and a bit unnerving. I set out shopping with some clients via FaceTime, as they walked the aisles of drug stores and grocery stores, pointing their phones in the direction of limited options for hair colouring on slightly bare shelves, helping them pick out shades and giving them strict instructions on how to apply the products once they were home. I was running personalized tutorials on how to mix colour how to trim your "fringe" and how to cut your husband's hair with whatever tools they had at their disposal. Never in my lifetime did I think that I would be watching in horror, as clients pulled out chunky scissors from junk drawers in kitchens, bathrooms, or home offices to use for a haircut to get people by in this unprecedented time! Colouring hair and other hair services are not a necessity in life, but you could have fooled me when salons around the world were shut down as a non-essential service!

This was one end of the spectrum. The other end was people suddenly finding themselves wanting to grow colour-treated hair to its natural state at a time when they were rarely seeing anyone. It made sense! The world was shut down and people were barely leaving their homes. When they did leave, their hair was often tied up, or tucked under a hat, partially to keep it safe from particles of virus potentially floating in the air. Faces were covered by masks. Not too many people were looking each other in the eyes when out and about, so it was a perfect time to take on this daunting task. Pre COVID19, clients who contemplated letting their hair grow out to its natural colour would get a list of options on how to do so from me. Some methods are costly, some require determination and patience. In the past, I have had a few clients that shaved their heads to remove all the colour-treated hair on their heads once they reached a growth of 1-1 ½ inches out of their scalp. They started a new style and colour from that point. This is not my favourite option, but effective for those who are bold enough to do so. Growing out colour-treated hair certainly requires a series of pep talks to get the client through all the "I can't take it anymore!" moments.

People sporting short haircuts suddenly found themselves willingly, and sometimes unwillingly, growing out their hair to a longer style. Fringes were being grown out, men in suits were suddenly donning longer, un-coiffed styles, and sometimes ponytails.

Towards the end of April 2020, the provincial government announced the soft re-opening of non-essential businesses, opening doors with restrictions, procedures, and protocols in place at the beginning of May. The thought of having people in my home again brought back some anxiety as this seemed to be too early for me. My new grandson, whom I was still visiting almost daily, was only one month old. I chose to stay closed for an additional month, opening again on June 6th, at which point, I had been closed for 12 weeks.

My clients came back to a freshly painted salon, now equipped with a new cabinet with doors for my retail product, the addition of new sealed containers to hold my towels and capes, and an air purification system with filters that needed to be replaced every six months. I now worked wearing a black uniform and wore both a mask and face shield. The amount of money that I spent to upgrade my new standards was ridiculous, heading towards a thousand dollars. I am a one-woman show! The mark-up of masks from suppliers had tripled in price from what they were before the pandemic. I couldn't imagine what larger salons had to invest to make their workspace COVID19 friendly, including partitions to separate workspaces. My clients were also required to enter my salon space with a mask, always covering their mouth and nose. No more offerings of coffee, tea or water were allowed.

I have several clients who are hearing impaired and must wear hearing aids. The addition of the mask, adding a tiny layer of elastic around the ear, which already supports the aids and a pair of glasses, created a challenge for many. Reading lips to aid in understanding the happenings of the world around them had been stripped from them. I now needed to wait until they were back at the station chair, with their artificial hearing devices in their ears before any type of communication could be had once their devices were removed for shampooing. I increased the volume of my already loud voice for them to understand.

Back in full swing, I found clients now explaining why they were sneezing, coughing, or clearing their throats while sitting in my chair. I was doing the same. One of my clients told me that if she didn't know that I suffered from various allergies, she would have run out of my salon as I was having a sneezing fit while doing her hair. Funny… and not funny. Conversations became fixated on the pandemic and how everyone was coping. I had an ongoing list of events, trips, parties, weddings, and other celebrations that were cancelled because of border closures and restrictions on how many people could gather in one place at one time. Funerals were being put on hold or being streamed for families to pay respects to loved ones. My list of cancellations included tickets for a rare and busy concert season for me, all between the dates of April the 4th and May the 5th. One concert date was a birthday present for my son, two tickets for us to spend an evening with the Winnipeg Symphony Orchestra who were set to perform the music of Led Zeppelin, the music that he loved to play when he was honing his skills as a drummer. Others were concerts by performers I had not seen before. Some I had seen before, and as a super fan, wanted to enjoy their music again. All five of these concerts were either postponed due to the pandemic or cancelled altogether. Plans were also in the beginning stages of organizing a 60th birthday party weekend for our graduating class for the summer of 2020. We are a rare group of fine individuals who have stayed connected heading into our senior years. Unfortunately, this event too would have to wait. One cancelled event that broke my heart was a trip with my girlfriends from British Columbia and our husbands, scheduled for the end of July. We were to head down to Nashville to celebrate our 60th birthday and had booked an exquisite three-bedroom condo, with plans to visit all the city's popular landmarks and hot spots. It was sad to have that moment in time pass us by without seeing each other.

As autumn arrived, people were quick to cancel appointments without hesitation if they had been advised of exposure to COVID19-positive friends or family, or at the sign of sniffles and coughs. I had my first COVID19 test in October, as the start of a cough appeared out of nowhere. Having this symptom prevented my husband from going to work so I needed proof that I did not have the virus for him to carry on as usual.

With numbers rising fast and furious, the Chief Medical Officer for our province announced that all non-essential businesses would be closed again, effective Thursday, November 12th, 2020. Our second industry lock-down. For the second time in my life, I was collecting a wage from a government support program. And for the first time in a thirty-four-year career, I would not be working during a busy Christmas season. I decorated my house that weekend, with no one other than my husband and me to appreciate my seasonal trinkets. It was the first time in thirty-three years that I did not see my children on Christmas morning, and I sorely missed seeing my grandkids to share my traditional homemade crêpes with the typical and usually partially frozen strawberries, amongst other brunch food to celebrate the season. The 26th of December, Boxing Day, a day celebrated the day after Christmas in Canada and by other Commonwealth countries, originated as a holiday to give gifts to the poor. Today, it is more known as a shopping day with great sales on items ranging from furniture to clothing, and of course, leftover decorations that were not purchased before the holidays. But for me, Boxing Day has always been my mother's birthday. When I was a child, I watched my mother spend her day in the kitchen, ensuring that everyone who came to our traditional open house had plenty of food and drink. It was never about her birthday. For her, it was about entertaining, gathering, love and laughter. She taught me long ago that the holiday season was always about spending time with family, friends, and loved ones. Never about gifts or extravagance. Time... one of the most treasured things in life. For the first time in my life, my family's traditional event on December 26th, 2020, was cancelled. Even after my mom's passing in 2006, I wanted to continue the tradition and offered our home as the "go-to" location. My mom's party continues annually to keep the family tradition alive. It includes a bad rendition of The Twelve Days of Christmas, usually sung off-key, and a homemade Mocha Cake, a recipe that hails from my dad's ancestors in France. This recipe is a take-it-or-leave-it kind of tradition, with most leaving it. The icing of this cake is made from a homemade custard, strong coffee and one pound of butter. (This is not a typo! One pound of butter.) The young ones normally shy away from it but the older folk in the family go back for seconds. I do not eat this cake, however, I am the one who makes it year after year. With the world around us sitting still on December 26th due to the pandemic, I baked the infamous cake and delivered quarters of it to each of my four sisters and their spouses.

With numbers of COVID19 cases slowly making their way down, giving our medical system some relief, our salons and other non-essential businesses were given the green light to re-open their doors in the last week of January 2021. After another eleven-week hiatus, I opened my salon on January 26th, adding a day to my normal three-day workweek to catch up. Aside from cooking, baking, and reading during this lock-down, I also took a serious look at my client base, noticing which ones had not come back from the initial lock-down. At this point, I realized that I had seven clients who decided to go natural as far as colouring their hair was concerned. They would no longer be needing that hair service. One client moved to another province to be with her daughter and young family after having lived through the provincial border closures, missing them terribly. Another sadly passed away from cancer. My already small-scale clientele was shrinking with no rationale other than the unusual circumstances during these unfamiliar times in our world. Additional days to my first few weeks back ended up giving me unwanted weeks off in a six-week cycle. My husband told me that I needed to hire myself a new booking agent! I was thankful to be where I was at in my work life and happy to have a husband whose career kept him working through all this turmoil. I could not help but think of all who were working in this industry, needing a steady income to live, needing the loyalty of their clientele to support them and help them survive these pause moments. Colleagues from around the world were commenting on social media platforms about the ill effects of the pandemic and how the closures had affected our industry and their personal lives. Some parts of the world had an initial lockdown which was much longer than the one we had here, and I often pondered on how interesting it was that we were all dealing with different scenarios.

Having turned 60 in March of 2020, I now became the Costco shopper, as the store offered senior hours from 8:00 to 9:00 am for people who were 60 years of age and older. You have no idea how thrilled I was to show my identification to be allowed entry, along with other people who, according to the staff at Costco "looked their age" though I did not. What does a 60-year-old look like? My husband who is one year my junior has gray hair and never got asked for ID when he became of age to shop at the senior hour. Is that the marker? Gray hair? The only bad thing about me doing the shopping was that I had to do all the heavy lifting myself, which isn't the best thing for my nasty back issues. As much as the world all hoped that 2021 would bring brighter days, unfortunately, it did not. With rising numbers again, we began another seven-week lockdown of non-essential business closures the week of May the 9th. Was there no end to this madness? After this third lock-down, I opened my doors again, in the last week of June. Only two weeks after my third pause in business, my husband and I went on a one-week camping trip with our new-to-us trailer that we purchased in the fall of 2020. I must admit, I felt guilty doing this after having had so much time off already in one year. We had booked three separate weeks to be away, just hours from the city limits so that we could experience the picturesque parks available to us in our beautiful province. My husband had worked through a very trying year, so we wanted to keep these get-away trips over the summer in our schedule. We discovered that camping, something that neither of us had done in years, was an old friend that took us to a complete state of relaxation. Enhanced by my new hammock and the chirping of many birds, the camping experience offered a tranquillity that I will not be giving up anytime soon. We fell in love with camping so much that we traded the used camper in for a new model and look forward to venturing out a little further with it from here on in.

At the beginning of the pandemic, a news anchor commented that we were all in the same storm, yet we were all in different boats. How accurate this statement was and continues to be today. There were so many unknowns about this virus at the beginning, and, at the time of writing this book, they continue to be present today, mutating into new and different variants, all words that were most certainly not part of my vocabulary before 2019. I continue to be vigilant for the sake of everyone in my family, specifically my little grandchildren who are not yet protected from its ill effects, and my clients who come into my home salon for hair services. Our industry cleaning practices are standard and have always been stern. When the pandemic hit, we all upped our game to meet new regulations and practices, yet I feel that our already stellar regimes were not altered too much to meet the protocols. We are a caring industry and do all that we can so that our clients have a positive experience and are safe in our salons.

My client who visited Vietnam at the beginning of 2020 survived her trip and survived her illness, though she still has symptoms that come to the forefront occasionally, causing her regular visits to her doctor. She was never formally diagnosed with the virus, but as her health continues to show signs of being a long-hauler, it is assumed that what plagued her while she was in Vietnam was, in fact, the COVID19 virus.

My grandson is healthy and celebrated his second birthday in March of 2022. He is a loving little brother to his big sister and life in their home is somewhat back to normal with kid activities in full swing.

Here are a few interesting tidbits:

In April of 1918, a pandemic hit known as the Spanish Flu. Most modern virologists and epidemiologists agree that this virus likely did not begin in Spain. This country was neutral during World War 1, a conflict that overlapped with this pandemic. Spain reported outbreaks of the virus to news organizations in the spring of 1918, whereas other countries involved in the war were unwilling to broadcast the toll that the flu was having on its troops and lack of supplies. Hence, the Spanish Flu.

A few months before this, at the end of December 1917, for me, a more important event happened... my mother was born. Three years later, my father was born in November 1920.

Fast forward one hundred years... twice. My granddaughter was born in 2017, 100 years after my mother's birth, and my grandson was born one week after the world shut down in 2020, during the pandemic of COVID19, 100 years after my father's birth. History eerily repeating itself.

I suspect that there will be many books written about this pandemic by medical professionals and people wanting to share their journeys. Live Your Life is a personal story written by Amanda Kloots. It is a real-life, sad story about the ill effects of this virus that killed her husband Nick Cordero in July 2020, but not before much heartache, which began in March 2020. Nick leaves behind his wife, Amanda, and beautiful baby boy, Elvis, as well as his extended family and friends. I feel that this book is a must-read. Or better yet, hear her emotion on Audible or your favourite audio provider.

What has been most difficult in the past two years is hearing stories of all my friends, clients, and other people close to me who work in the medical field. They have put in long hours of work at our hospitals and medical clinics and walk through life completely exhausted. I cringe when I hear pleas for help as our critical care systems fail due to a shortage of staff. And I cringe for all the sick. Our hospitals have beds filled with COVID19 patients, yet the ones who suffer from heart ailment, broken limbs, car accident victims, organ issues and cancers also need the attention of medical professionals. Across this country, thousands of surgeries have been pushed back while medical personnel are deployed to new tasks to accommodate those sick with the virus. It is simply wearing our medical professionals out.

No one knows when this is going to end. So, for now, it is what it is. I never felt that my rights were being denied as this worldwide pandemic was being managed, and would like to believe that any leader in power did what they needed to do to keep us all safe. It truly is a phenomenon, an event that one is likely to experience only once in a lifetime, and all we can do is our best to stay safe and hope that 2022 will bring this pandemic to a place of normalcy.

Be kind and be well everyone.

"As you grow older, you will discover that you
have two hands, one for helping yourself, the
other for helping others." *Audrey Hepburn*

What Scissors Taught Me

The Canadian Hairstyling curriculum is broken down into eight sections comprised of Occupational Skills, Hair and Scalp, Cutting, Styling, Chemical Services, Hair Colour, Specialized Services and Salon Operations. When I took my course thirty-five years ago, a lot of time was dedicated to personal well-being and health. The Van Dean Manual was a popular industry teaching tool created by the Milady Publishing Corporation. It was first published in 1940, revised in 1976 and re-printed in 1987, which was a brand spanking new edition when I started school in the same year. This textbook is now simply known as Milady. There were clearly laid-out opportunities for young women and men to flourish in the industry. The first three chapters offered tips on proper hygiene and good grooming, visual poise, and personality development. Sub-sections touched on personal hygiene, public safety, balanced diet, dealing with the fatigue and what well-groomed female and male cosmetologists should look like, down to hairstyle, clothes, facial make-up, jewelry and shoes that work and don't work. "Males: Moustache or beard must be trimmed and styled. Trim hair in nostrils." Let's continue with balancing your body weight for good posture to lessen back strain in both standing and sitting positions. The manual even touched upon normal and weak foot arches, attitude, behaviour and proper use of vocabulary. "Thinking should be part of your personality," it promoted. "If you want people to listen when you speak, think clearly and then communicate your thoughts as interestingly as you can. Use a pleasant voice, be emotionally stable... realize what a great beautifier serenity is and strive for emotional balance." The book promoted being gracious, polite, and having a sense of humour. "Your voice is you! The voice should convey sincerity, intelligence, friendliness, vitality, flexibility, and expressiveness." Chapter three ended with directions on how to have "conversational charm" and a list of topics not to discuss, more specifically, your own personal problems, religion, another patron's poor behaviour, your love affairs, your own financial status, poor workmanship of fellow workers, your own health problems and information given to you in confidence. Quite the list!

How do I remember all of this you ask? I still have the book! I've never been able to let it go. I hoard what I love! This includes a collection of old mannequin heads that were displayed on shelves in my basement, startling my teenage kids when they would make their way in that direction. Now they are the best, life-sized dolls for my granddaughter to play with, which I'm sure her little friends would be envious of if they knew they existed.

Thank goodness there is more leniency towards everyone being themselves in the workplace. I know a few barbers who would have struggled with the conservative thought regarding beards and moustaches. Today, there is also a better focus on mental health awareness. The suggestions and basic human behaviours taught in this manual can help you live healthy regardless of your career choice. We are all capable of and should strive for, a little bit of kindness in our daily activities.

Once you jump into the hair cutting portion of the curriculum, you learn about the basic and necessary tools that you will need for this skillset, which is a large part of this chosen trade. As you begin your career, your tool kit is quickly enhanced by purchasing trendy irons, expensive blow dryers, and other "necessary" tools to better your services, and most certainly include multiple pairs of scissors. Some professionals become "scissor slingers" with fancy manoeuvring techniques that I have yet to, and likely will never, master. Palming the scissors and comb, a technique taught right out of the textbook and in schools has always worked for me. With my luck, if I tried to get any fancier than that, my scissors would go flying out of my grip, injuring a client or myself, or breaking something in my surroundings. I am always fascinated by platform artists that can quickly and easily reach for a sharp object like a cowboy reaching for his gun in an old western, bringing their instruments back to resting mode in their hand and making it look like a breeze. School teaches us that there are many options at our disposal to use to cut hair, scissors being the most obvious one. There are, however, many other tools available to perfect a look, various styles of razors, barber and thinning shears, clippers, and trimmers to name a few. As time goes on in your career, you find your favourite brand, size and style.

School identifies for us every part of the haircutting scissor: the moving point, the moving blade, the pivot and screw, the finger grip, the finger brace (also known as the tang,) the still point, the still blade, the cutting edges, the shank, and the thumb grip. Yes, these are all parts of a simple pair of scissors. Hairstyling scissors are specific, in the same way that pinking shears used in sewing are specific to cutting fabric with a zigzag edge. Hairstyling and barber scissors are meant to cut hair, which is similar to fabric, as hair comes in different colours, textures, and densities. Hairstyling scissors come in various styles, some with swivel thumb holes, offset styles or straight, and vary drastically in investment costs.

They could be cast, meaning the metal is melted down, poured into a mould, and then cooled to take on its new shape, potentially creating a tiny pinhole in the scissor. This is the reason why hairdressers have a tiny moment of despair should they, unfortunately, drop their scissors, as there is then the potential for the pinhole to cause the scissors to break or cause a chip in the fragile blades. Scissors could also be forged, which is the process of working metal into shape by hammering or pressing metal at 2,100 to 2,300 degrees Fahrenheit. This expands the molecular structure of the steel so that the molecules may move when struck by a heavy object to form the scissors. Scissors used in the salon are not your average pair of scissors. Instructors warn us of their sharpness. No one ever really warns us, however, that you can take off some serious amounts of knuckle skin with them if you're not paying close attention. I guess it's a learn as you go philosophy. I can guarantee you that every hairstylist has, at one time or another, felt the sharpness of the blades come together with their knuckle in between them, and the instinct is not to continue with that snip! Yet I cannot tell you how many times I have caught my knuckles in that position, my brain telling me to continue with the cut, pushing harder, resulting in drawing a lot of blood. This is one good reason to have a well-stocked first-aid kit in a hair salon.

Scissors. They sit in my holster for daily use, some are tucked away in a drawer of spares or has-beens. They are the tools that have created a connection between me and every single one of my clients over the last thirty-five years and counting. They are the items that have given me the ability to do my job the best way I know how. They are the device that I use to take the hair off when I need to freshen up a look, enhance a trend, change a style completely, cut, blend, shape and create. Create! Such a wonderful word! Hairstylists sometimes call scissors by a different name, like snippers, if only to ease little people into trusting the process. Adding soothing words of encouragement or calming dialogue while snipping away can also help, especially while taking someone to a short style before cancer treatments. Scissors become our babies. They need to be oiled, sharpened periodically, constantly cleaned, and disinfected, with tender loving care, always.

In the fall of 1999, I had a new guest come into the salon, referred to me by one of my long-time clients. As soon as we returned to my station after her initial consultation and shampoo, she announced that she would be leaving me in five years. For a short minute, I wondered if she was terminally ill, or had a plan to move out of the province in five years. I found it to be an odd statement when she had no idea how this visit would end. If she didn't like the way I was doing things, would she stick it out with me anyway, and if she really loved me at the end of the term, would she really leave? Both of us turned 39 that year and we hit it off immediately and began a cherished relationship. She introduced me to her husband and daughters, who also became valued guests in my chair in that time frame. In December of 2003, having moved her appointment several weeks to accommodate her scheduled holiday party season, her overdue cut and colour appointment ended up being two weeks later than usual. On this blizzardy Saturday, just before the noon hour, I was coming toward the door to greet her when I had been looking for her through the large picture window and saw her walking from her car through the storm. A powerful gust of wind helped her open the door to the very busy salon packed with clients and stylists, where she announced loudly, "I cut my bangs!" as she entered the salon. I'm not sure that she was aware of how loud this proclamation was, but loud it was, and it made everyone inside the salon turn to look in her direction. I burst out laughing as she made her way through the crowded entrance. There was no need for the declaration! Her own scissors had taken her fringe an inch above her eyebrows! Baby bangs... a cute fashion on many if done right. Oh boy! She apologized for cutting her hair and not having the patience to wait for her appointment.

It's funny how people feel a need to apologize for creating new hairstyles on their own heads with their own kitchen scissors. The sink chair or the hydraulic chair usually becomes the confessional where guests divulge the happenings of their hair mishaps, not the reception area of the salon. This was a first. Holiday season 2004 was the last time that I saw this beauty in my chair, as her five-year promise had arrived. True to her word, she moved on. This was a sad "see you later." She had presented me with various gifts over the years, some for no reason at all, and that particular season, she gave me a playful ornamental acrylic snowman on skates that toggles back and forth from one skate to the other, appearing as though he is skating on ice. He still adorns my living room every Christmas as a beautiful reminder of her kindness. My kids used to play with it when they were young, and now, it is my grand-children who topple him over and keep him company during the holiday season.

I am a lover of Oprah and subscribe to her website. My sub-scription includes occasional emails full of good suggestions for leisurely reading. Recently included in one of those emails was a video link to an Oprah Winfrey Show recorded in 2003, talking about the best Christmas of Oprah's life. She tells the story of a time when she lived with her mother, on welfare. Her mother announced that they were not going to have Christmas that year because they couldn't afford it. And then, three nuns showed up. They showed up with a doll for her and some food. This became her best Christmas ever because somebody remembered her, and she wasn't going to be the kid that received nothing. As an adult with an amazing career and astounding financial success, Oprah and her team organized a trip to South African orphanages to deliver gifts for each child, with tags on each present, bearing every one of the children's names. In handing out the gifts, Oprah documents that it could be seen in their eyes that they felt remembered... that someone cared about them... that at that moment, they mattered.

That's how I want my clients to feel. I want EVERYONE to feel like SOMEONE!

Clients have many choices when it comes to receiving personal services. There are salons of all sizes on every block in the suburbs of most cities, which gives people numerous options for choosing a hairstylist. There are many reasons that someone new walks through your doors. Perhaps they were referred to the salon by an existing client or recommended by a friend. They may have moved from another city and walked through your doors by chance. Maybe they were leaving the salon that they were at because they weren't satisfied with either their past stylist or the environment of the salon. The point is, once someone sits in your chair, it now becomes your job as a stylist to keep them there.

My career has been a beautiful journey. Every single day that I am working, I wonder whether it is my client that is going to have the best experience that day or is it going to be me? An appointment gone well is when both my client and I feel as though we have been cared for and that we matter. I feel that there is much that people don't know or understand about this career. Even hairstylists underrate themselves. Instinctively, when asked what we do for a living, many reply with, "I'm just a hairdresser." The word just needs to be removed from that response. Dr. Lew Losoncy, one of my many industry mentors, a psychologist who studied the art of hairstyling and the human connection that exists between stylist and client, had the best response to this. At one point in my life, I even owned a sweatshirt that had his saying on it.

"I cosmetically and psychologically transform self-images and destinies of fellow human beings." Now there is a fabulous job description!

I have had some hardships along the way as many of us do in our careers, and I handled them well enough to get me where I am today. Even though there have been some trying times, my scale tips substantially to the side of gratitude and happiness. My clients have blessed me with many physical gifts over the years that I still treasure today. Their greatest gifts are the moments when they walked through my salon doors and sat in my chair, allowing me the opportunity to share my talents, most often while holding a pair of scissors. The relationships that we have created together have been my precious gift. Their presence, and not presents, is what has given me the unexpected longevity in an industry that I love beyond words. Wayne Dyer once said, "Doing what you love is the cornerstone of having abundance in your life." I have had many blessings in my life, and the day I decided to become a hairstylist, abundance filled my world even more.

What scissors taught me is that it's not about the scissors. It's not about the haircut or the colour or the highlights. I was taught that good enough is not good enough, and to learn to perfect your skills as a hairstylist. Yet, I can assure you that almost every one of my clients can attest to my imperfectness. Heck, I have even had some come back a day after their appointments for me to straighten out an unwanted asymmetrical haircut. That's when I know that there was a seriously needed conversation going on with either a lot of emotion or a lot of laughter, or both.

The world lost actor Betty White on December 31st, 2021. She was seventeen days shy of her one-hundredth birthday. Her career was plentiful and loved by multiple generations. Ryan Reynolds' tribute to her was very fitting when he said, "She managed to grow very old and somehow, not old enough." Each role that she undertook was superbly represented. One of my favourite roles was the one she had on The Golden Girls. The theme song "Thank You for Being a Friend" was written by Andrew Gold for this series, which makes me smile because (1) it makes me think of Betty and (2) it wholeheartedly represents what scissors taught me most of all. If you take a chance on the strangers that walk through your door the same way that they take a chance on you, innumerable relationships can be created, leading to a very long career in the trade of hairstyling. A stranger always has the potential to become a friend. To you, my dear clients, past and present, thank you for being a friend.

"Hairdressers are a wonderful breed. You work one-on-one with another human being and the object is to make them feel so much better and to look at themselves with a twinkle in their eye." *Vidal Sassoon*

From the Bottom of My Heart...

Between the life lived while preparing for this dream of mine, and the procrastination it took to sit down and write, this book would have never come to fruition without the following giants in my life...

Gilles, my wonderful husband. I'm not sure you knew what you were signing up for when you met me. Your easy-going way of living life balances my crazy, which makes us the unique team that we have become. Without even trying, you became a wonderful stepdad to my children and with their acceptance of you in their lives, you have now graduated to becoming the best Pépère that any grandchild could ever ask for. Thank you for tagging along on all my crazy rides, with love, support and encouragement. And of course, your set of teacher's eyes was much appreciated catching those little mistakes that weren't caught on any of the dozens of re-reads of these pages, making this book possible. J't'aime b'en gros, chéri amour. XO

Samantha and Tanner, my amazing children. This book cover is because of your genius! Thanks, Sam, for your idea and strands of hair, and Tanner, thank you for all the information on inviting colours for book covers. Your marketing and project management backgrounds gave you the knowledge to watch over me as I created my new social media platforms for my new endeavour, not that you asked to be involved. Thank you so much for stepping forward when I needed your help. You two have put up with many of my shenanigans over your lifetime, not always in accordance with my actions, I know, yet I still feel your love and acceptance for who I am. I appreciate our mutual respect. I must have done something good in my life to have deserved the gift of you two beautiful souls. I love you both, more than you will ever know. Thank you for bringing Craig, Cassidy, Liam, Chelsea, and of course, Finn and Brady into my world. You all fill my cup with so much love and happiness. XO

My mom and dad blessed me with four older sisters who somewhat became "additional mothers" to me throughout my life… Claudette, Lorraine, Louise, and Terry. You are a gift to me! You have blessed me with four of mom's favourite sons-in-law, nine nieces and nephews and their lovely families. We are one fantastic bunch. XO

A very special and honourable mention to my sister Terry. THANK YOU are two small words for all the time you spent on this project with me. You gave me the final kick that I needed to get it off and running. Your teachings on page breaks, re-wording, too, many, commas, in, my, writing, helped me to get this book in decent shape. Your inspiration, feedback, support and many edits were all necessary for this dream to become a reality. I am eternally grateful. XO

In 2006, I walked into one of my evening courses while completing my Vocational Teaching certification. The woman sitting next to me was pleasant, but we didn't say much to each other.

During round-table introductions, I introduced myself and could feel this woman's eyes beam into me. She immediately turned to me and said, "My name is Sherry, I am an esthetician by trade, and you and I need to get to know each other, girl!" We have been friends ever since. We even worked on our Bachelor of Education together. Thank you so much for spending four days of your life working on my final edits. Your expert eyes to finish the task was much needed. I appreciate you and am ever so thankful that our paths have crossed! XO

Larry, Larry T, Pops, thank you for your years of love and friendship. When I shared with you that I was writing a book, your first question to me was if there was going to be any mention of you in it, and the answer is, yes indeed. You were a very big part of my young adulthood and my beginning successes as a salon owner. Of course, you continue to be a big part as we walk through this life together with our kids and grandkids. We are the Canadian version of Demi Moore and Bruce Willis. You will always be in my books, my friend. XO

Yvette, my warrior with an unstoppable spirit. The luck of us being in elementary school together at the same time was not a coincidence. We continuously nurture ourselves the way that we do, living the greatest bonus of friendship that life has to offer. It doesn't matter how much or how little we see each other, as we both know that we are always there for each other. Don't ever leave me, my friend. I need you! XO

Nicole, thank you for allowing me to share your mother's name and expose the great friendship I had with her on these pages. Sharing her beauty and our special bond was important to me. I am ever so grateful for being permitted to tell the world about her angelic life perspective. XO

Joanne. Neighbours by chance, friends by choice. I am so happy that our parents struck up a friendship so long ago. I was a one-year-old when you were born, and my older sisters babysat you. I honestly don't remember sending that dreaded wooden swing into your face when we were kids, scarring your eye for life. It was likely a subconscious ploy to brand my mark on you so that you never forget about me. Thank you for introducing me to your wonderful husband Lester, who is a shared soul on many of these pages. Your family has provided much content for this book. That being said, I likely have enough material for a sequel. I wish that everyone was blessed to have friends like you in their lives. XO

This industry throws you into many situations where people mentor and inspire you. For me, Wayne Grund was one of those people. THANK YOU, Wayne, for taking time out of your busy show season to read my manuscript. You live on these pages as your teachings influenced many of my decisions throughout my career. You are a gift, my friend. XO

Shelley, my girl! A lot of who I am as a hairstylist is because of your mentorship and friendship. You and I have travelled together around the sun for the last twenty-three years. We have shared many great moments, with my all-time favourites, storytelling in countless hotel rooms together, or in each other's houses. Thank you, kindred spirit. I look forward to our continued friendship, wherever that may take us. XO

Natasha, dear girl! From the other side of the ocean, you provided me with the title that I was frantically looking for and needed to replace the one that I no longer felt was usable. Your loving push was felt in the most heartwarming ways, all the way from Spain to Canada. I can't wait until the day we meet face to face. You are a gem! Thank you! XO

Last, and most certainly not the least, to all my clients… you grace me with your presence every time you sit in my chair for a hair service. To those that have continually trusted me with your heads in my hands, to those who have modelled for me at hair shows and those who allowed me to play with your hair and photograph you during my competition days… each one of you has filled my soul with so many feelings, so much beauty. You have taught me lessons, given me challenges, brought me around the world with you in your adventures, and taught me too many things to list. We have shared happy times and sad times. We have celebrated, we have cried and we have laughed uncontrollably. I give each one of you my heartfelt THANK YOU, for allowing me to continue in this industry that I have loved since childhood. I could never have imagined that my career would last this long, and suffice it to say, that none of it would have been possible without YOU! XO

In parting, I offer you these words from the gift of Michael O'Brien's Pause, Breathe, and Reflect Meditation

May you see the abundance in your life,
May you live in harmony and in peace,
May you allow your days and moments to unfold with grace,
May you have the strength to endure and to let go of what no longer serves you,
May you be healthy, May you be safe,
May you feel seen, May you feel heard, May you feel loved.
With much love... Denise

About the Author

Denise Létienne has thirty-five years of experience as a hairstylist, salon owner, platform artist, and independent stylist. What Scissors Taught Me is her first book. She has her Red Seal Certification in Hairstyling, Adult and Vocational Teaching Certification, and a Bachelor of Education. When she's not behind the chair, you can find her reading, knitting, walking, practicing yoga, and writing.

She lives in her hometown of Winnipeg, Manitoba with her wonderful husband. She enjoys spending time with her two adult children, their spouses, her grandchildren, and two grand dogs. Look for her account dedicated to What Scissors Taught Me on Instagram.

Printed in Canada